To thine own self, be true.

AS I SEE IT

VOLUME I: BUSINESS

Phoenix Normand

I dedicate this book to two of the strongest women I've ever known.

My mother, Myra Callaway and my late grandmother, Mary Lee Marsh.

To my mother, you're my best friend, my daily inspiration, my moral compass, and the sole reason I exist on this earth.

You're a cancer survivor. An inspiration to all you come into contact with. You have the biggest, most resplendent pair of wings waiting at Heaven's Gate upon your arrival. Don't rush to get them, tho. I still need you here!

To my grandmother, thanks for being the father my father could never be. Thanks for your special kind of wisdom and the BS-free delivery that has now become my signature.

You taught me how to fight, fists and wits. Your legacy lives on through me. Well done, Lady.

To my ex-bosses, mentors, and teachers: Sangita Verma, Farhad Mohit, Robert Hanson, You Nguyen, Adam Lindemann, Alex Brousset, Marnell and Norine Xavier, Paula Case, Ronnie Reddick, Ledisi, Delton Starlon, Sharon Jarmon, Anne Oliver, Frank Castaldini, Erin O'Hare, Maria Nardi-Leon, Nadine Fontana, Steve McSween, Bobby Hernandez, and Jeff Alvarez.

I am who I am and where I am because you believed in me and selflessly paid it forward. I strive each day to make you proud of me.

To my besties, trīb, and significant exes, thanks for being in my life to teach me the lessons the Universe sent you to teach. I love you.

To my haters, FUCK YOU. I'm a published author now.

4

Table of Contents

FOREWORD

Writing this book has been a pain in the ass! There, I said it. THE TRUTH. I have not enjoyed the process at all. The numerous starts and stops. The constant re-reads and re-writes. The doubts, frustrations, insecurities and all of the childhood crap this torturous process unearthed I would trade for a karate chop right between my eyeballs any day of the week.

"But, why?" you may ask. I mean most authors talk about their numerous catharses and surrendering to the process and all of this glorious, transcendency. I don't buy a single word of it. If I could count how many times my expensive ass laptop almost became a frisbee due to lack of inspiration or words coming out of me that I've never even used before. I've walked away from this book so many times over the past few years I could classify as a bad father. I have no kids, by the way.

Writing this book exposed me to an entirely new type of discipline for which I was not prepared. Like, at all. You must make time to write. And when you do eventually find that time you must let it control you vs. you controlling it. Otherwise, it doesn't work. Words don't get said in the way you usually say them. You start overthinking and doing stupid shit like trying to sound smarter than you are. (Draft #2). And you become more and more frustrated and worried that you'll never finish or that your audience will start reading and immediately lose interest.

After re-reading the first two drafts of this book, I quickly realized that I hated them. They just weren't me. I write so freely on LinkedIn and my numerous other socials. It naturally flows out of me and immediately onto the page. As a result, I have amassed a growing audience of voracious readers who claim they can't get enough. And I can't supply enough because I've been too busy writing and re-writing this bloody book numerous times!

Since you're reading this, Stella clearly re-found her groove and the natural flow of words has returned. I'm writing from the same headspace as I write on LinkedIn and I'm actually funny and blatantly honest again. Not contrite and weird.

The biggest epiphany was a simple concept that has now become a battle cry for me. Tell the whole truth. Unabashedly. Once I stopped wrestling with my thoughts and allowing myself to be sabotaged by societal pressures, insistent

"Where's the book?!" emails and DMs, and merely telling it like it is, in my own time, it all just flowed. I felt no anxiety. In fact, I felt empowered. Something about telling the whole truth just sets you free. You no longer care what anyone thinks because the truth is unequivocal.

My grandmother used to say, "Opinions are like assholes. Everybody has one and they're mostly full of shit." Man, do I miss her.

When writing this book, I kept that phrase in mind. This book is one, big-ass, opinion piece. My opinion. It's an opinion derived from over 27 years as a top-performing, C-suite Executive Assistant, fortunate enough to experience more in my professional career than most people could ever fathom. I've been front-and-center for some of the most important business deals on the planet. I've sat next to Presidents, dignitaries, celebrities, and leaders who have addressed me by name and likely commented on some element of my style or attention-to-detail at an event I've thrown or meeting I've booked. I've supported executives who have changed the world in some easily quantifiable way. I've even worked on hack week projects that have become the apps we use every single day as yet another example of the casual ubiquity in all of our lives.

It's been a fantastic ride, but it hasn't always been an easy one. As a bit of a risk-taker I've managed to get myself into some pretty gnarly situations supporting both amazing and bat-shit crazy executives and teams. I've had as many failures as successes. Probably more of the former. But they've all converged into a life that has been filled with global adventures, uncertainty, curiosity, near-death experiences, wonder and pride, especially helping the executives I've supported succeed in bringing their ideas and dreams to life and watching the world adopt many of the products and services I've had some small part in helping to create and bring to market. It's a life and career lived to the fullest, bumps, bruises and all.

INTRODUCTION

This book is about my experience in business. My truth. AS I SEE IT. My viewpoint is a bit different from the plethora of CEO-penned how-to books and autobiographies in the wild. It's from the perspective of a Black, gay, 50-year-old, male Executive Assistant who has spent the majority of my professional career making others successful. I've had a front row seat for two dot-coms, numerous bull and bear markets, every possible legal and not-so-legal transaction ever completed and have mastered executives' personalities from obtuse and clueless to genius and borderline psychotic with grace. Because it's what I was paid to do and, eventually, grew to love.

Executive Assistants in business have historically been relegated to the shadows. We've always been viewed as the help even though the job advertisements of late read quite differently. We are professional martyrs. Simple as that. And have been so for decades in this role. And while this may seem like every reason to run screaming in the opposite direction, this role provides a level of access that is unparalleled within the company. Even the C-suite's aggregate access and influence within an organization pales in comparison to that of their Executive Assistants. Though we typically operate in the shadows we infiltrate absolutely every level of the business, internally and externally. In aggregate, we are an inimitable force within the global business community and can literally bring the business world to a screeching halt in minutes by combining our respective powers and influence should you really piss us off. Yes, you should be VERY afraid.

I have watched business change over the past 27 years. Some changes have been dramatic. Some things haven't changed much at all. C-suites still look pretty much the same as they did when I jumped into the Assistant pool. Still mostly male. Still mostly White. Still mostly (socially) clueless. But still really, really good at making the decisions that continue to move business and innovation forward and evolving the world in some way, every day.

This book is "business in the front, party in the back." I've included some very specific stories about my professional and personal lives, centered around my experiences as a C-suite Executive Assistant. My goal isn't to roast anyone's balls, only to call out the specific situations and, at times, people who've played a particular part in the story. To some this may seem like a bit of a digression from a business book and more of a tawdry autobiography that went off the rails somewhere. And, to an extent, it is. Happy to admit it.

I wasn't sure about how to write a book that told the whole story and provided enough context into why I've come to many of my conclusions in this book. Plus, I'm too young to write an autobiography, so there's that. After numerous starts and stops over the years, I reasoned the best way to do it was to include the stories and the specific lessons learned, hoping they would be entertaining enough to feed the curious among you and evoke a chuckle or two at the absolute absurdity and insanity I've faced throughout my career as an EA, but also provide some much-needed color and context missing from today's rah-rah business books, blogs and poorly shot, up-the-nose videos of perceived business experts ruling the socials. My hope is that it will allow others who may be making some of the same mistakes and poor decisions I've made or experiencing similar outcomes and not understanding why, to have something to reference to help change their situation or find that bit of validation missing from their individual struggles.

This book is mainly about business, inside the walls, and nothing too macro. Admittedly, I do bitch quite a bit in this book, but my ultimate goal is to provide solutions or ideas for solutions that truly could work if given a chance. Hopefully, it will spark more active, honest dialogue about the realities of today's business and those on those warnings on the horizon we blithely choose to ignore. These ideas are derived from personal experience and what has either worked before or could possibly work based on years of seeing companies, Boards, and executives make the same mistakes again and again. As I see it, business needs to start telling the truth about what it is, its motivations, its ineptitudes, its challenges and, most importantly, its end game. My intent with this book is to grab some shoulders and shake a few people into full consciousness. More importantly, hold up a rather large mirror in front of the business community so that we can truly look at ourselves, faults and all, and eventually be okay with what we all see. We're not there yet. But I believe we can get there if we make the time and expend the effort. And, for me, that starts with telling the whole truth. AS I SEE IT.

Chapter One:
It's About the Business

The Business Game of Thrones

Remember, Facebook was founded by an idea thief and opportunist. And I'm not even mad about it.

As much as we love to glorify the genius and success of Mark Zuckerberg, for whom I have tremendous though guarded respect, Facebook was not his idea. It was an idea originally conceived by Cameron and Tyler Winklevoss who'd hired him to help build out their networking idea while attending their respective universities. Zuck saw an opportunity to take that idea, build something even cooler and proceeded to co-opt it as his own. If you've read the history of Facebook and Mark Zuckerberg, you'll know this isn't old news. However, I believe we've allowed ourselves to conveniently forget that this was, essentially, one of the most crafty business idea heists of all time that is constantly overlooked, especially as we are now roasting his rather large balls over the flame regarding user information security, nefarious hacking, and the homogenized, Kool-Aid guzzling culture within the company he built into ubiquity. Remember, we all opted in. Willingly. As they say in my 'hood, "Don't hate the playa, hate the game."

Business is a game. I actually see it as frighteningly analogous to professional football. I'll explain.

There's a league full of owners. Those owners have teams. Those teams have coaches who recruit and oversee a group of players and issue the strategies and plays that are hopefully successful against the competition when executed by the players. The very best players are recruited and hired for the specific positions they play within the team. Everyone on the team, including the support staff (assistant coaches, trainers, even the water boy) are there to support the players in performing to the very best of their abilities while on the field. There are rules, referees, and an adoring public who are all-in as long as the team keeps winning. Owners, less so when the team starts losing, consistently. When teams start losing personnel changes are made, often overnight and with little-to-no warning. Players are benched for fresher backups looking for their chance to shine. Sometimes coaches lose their jobs because they can't pull their individual superstars together in such a way as to create the cohesion needed to win against their opponents each week. Sometimes they can't command the respect of those superstars and they are replaced by those who can. Players, often ill-prepared for the newfound money, fame, and responsibility make bonehead missteps that lead to poor performance, tank team morale, get them suspended, traded, or expelled from the league. Sometimes they get injured and aren't able to perform to the same standard and expectation as when they were hired. It's all pretty intricate and fascinating when you strip it down to the studs.

Business, as a whole, is really no different. In fact, business shares the same underlying themes and motivations: money, power, and the quest for legacy and ubiquity. And like football, the stakes are high and based almost solely on a team's ability to win consistently and, thus, bring in profits.

CEOs: The New Breed

There is a new breed of CEO finally emerging. They are much younger than the legacy CEOs currently ruling the roost. They likely lucked their way to the top spot by inventing the next big thing while slogging away in the trenches as an Engineer and vowing to do things differently if given the opportunity. They're likely well-educated, but not necessarily Stanford, Penn, or Harvard grads. And they've likely been socialized enough to understand, empathize with, and empower the minority populations at their companies, and be less compelled to perpetuate the numerous inequities endured by them at their previous companies. They are the future. Thank God.

However, they are emerging during a time of great change. The legacy CEOs still have all of the power and connections the new breed needs. Which means they are forced to travel in the same packs, engage in conversations that likely make their skin crawl, and often lean on the old guard for sage advice regarding their companies that, unfortunately, continue to perpetuate the same behaviors and ignorance complicit with putting profits squarely above the overall well-being of their employees.

With all of the poor behavior coming to light in the media by legacy CEOs and the innate desire to make tons of money, cash out, but also to do the right thing, the new breed are often caught in similar moral struggles between profits and doing what's morally and socially right.

Newer CEOs often suffer from a complete lack of management skills and are thrown into the deepest end of the pool, expected to swim perfectly. And they've likely recruited a number of their buddies who helped to manifest their must-have product who, also, have no idea what the fuck they're doing besides writing code for 14 hours a day.

Take Mark Zuckerberg for example. The Facebook leadership team was comprised mostly of roommates and fellow schoolmates who had zero management experience, little if any actual work experience, and thrown into a position of immense responsibility and power that grew exponentially with each new iteration of the company. I spoke with Zuck's very first Executive Assistant at an EA conference many years ago and she admitted that it was bedlam at times and that she quickly became equal parts "Mom" and moral compass for Zuck, his leadership team, and the company and helped create and maintain the cultural guidelines within which the company operated.

The process of going from idea to product, product to startup, then startup to funded company is a pretty singular focus for a new CEO, which often results in little to no attention paid to the thoughtful, cultural and experiential composition of the company. When you take funding and give up shares of your company the rules change. And the pressure to perform increases exponentially. As I see it, many new breed CEOs become overwhelmed by all of the responsibilities, expectations, and new, expert voices in the mix and simply go with the flow of traffic directed by the VCs they've collected money from. And therein lies the problem.

It's imperative for the new breed to be much more proactive pulling an advisory team together that perfectly aligns with their ethos, who can suggest additional team members early in the maturation of the company who are experienced and conditioned, and who can help to build a team that is talented and inclusive of everyone within the business community, not just the people who look like them, attended the same schools, or travel in the same packs.

A CEO's Focus

Newsflash: CEOs do not have it all figured out. In fact, many CEOs don't know their ass from a hole in the ground when they first start out. If you were fortunate enough to come up during the first dot-com boom, you'll know exactly what I'm talking about. Many CEOs are light on management skills, at best. Most lack evolved social skills. I've supported many who were previously obtuse-as-fuck Engineers who happened upon a great idea and, voila! They're magically CEOs! That 3-letter title carries a ton of weight, expectation, and often, misperception. People automatically assume that anyone with the CEO title has attended some magical CEO University in the town of Badass, Connecticut and can hit the ground sprinting once the freeway sign reads Palo Alto, California. Um, sorry to disappoint you. It's not even the case.

As I see it, CEOs have a very condensed set of objectives when they decide to take the leap and start a company. Something like the following:

Quickly move from concept to final product.

Build a dream team to help run the company.

Find and mine relevant industry connections.

Get customers.

Make money and build credibility as a must-have product.

IPO, sell, and move on to next idea.

These are really the only things CEOs are thinking about as they prepare to bring their big idea into the light. Sadly, once they start checking off a number of these items, they get blindsided by the realities of loading a bunch of stray animals (i.e., employees) onto the ark. Issues like:

Company morale

Meeting overload

Lack of time, especially for friends and family

Constant overwhelm

Leadership pissing contests

Team diversity issues and metrics

Given that CEO University doesn't actually exist, dealing with people in quantities larger than the frat they pledged to is truly a daunting endeavor. Dealing with emotions, frequent challenges to their knowledge or authority, making big decisions with unknown effects, answering to a

Board of Directors who intimidate the fuck out of them, etc. are situations even the best universities can't prepare them for.

I amend my previous statement. CEOs are often thrown into the deepest end of the ocean, not just the pool. They are often losing their shit while doing their best to learn as much as they can, take calculated risks, appear to be in complete control, and keep their marriages and friendships from completely falling apart, all while trying to fulfill that dream they had in the shower that one morning. Let's cut them some slack, shall we?

The CEO and Leadership Team

The CEO/Leadership Team dynamic has been one that I've witnessed up close for over two decades. I've seen amazing versions of this dynamic and I've seen abysmal ones. I can confidently say, the success of the company rides on the success of this dynamic, almost exclusively.

As I talk about in another section, one of the CEO's main goals is to source and assemble a kickass team to help run the company. These are typically experts in their respective fields who possess specific strengths or connections the CEO may lack or may not have the bandwidth to focus on. CFOs have a very specific role and have likely mastered all-things-financial in order to earn the title. CTOs have very specific technical expertise and the ability to keep all-things-technical on the rails for companies large and small.

Bringing these professionals together and getting them on the same page is often more difficult than finding them in the wild. They usually arrive with years of relevant experience, are convinced they know what works based on their previous successes and begin unzipping and whipping out appendages to make sure that everyone in the room knows they belong there. As an EA witnessing this time and time again, I still find it equal parts comical and ri-dick-ulous. Pun intended.

The success of a Leadership Team truly rests on the clarity of the vision of the CEO. First-time and newer CEOs often struggle with this as they haven't yet found the confidence and their voice to clearly state their vision. Often, they lack the self-awareness and vulnerability to admit that they simply aren't 100% sure about the process of getting to that vision. This will typically manifest in baseless edicts, "squirrel? squirrel?" changes to well-baked plans, or siloed thinking and behavior rendering the Leadership Team essentially useless until the vision or message is shared.

Transparency of thought and action is everything for a successful Leadership Team. Without it there is no opportunity for true cohesion. Each Leadership Team member needs to be crystal clear on the vision of the CEO and acutely aware of what the other leaders are communicating to their teams. Creating OKRs and KPIs together that support the ultimate vision of the CEO is what set the tone and plays for the rest of the organization. More often than not, I've seen this process go horribly because the CEO isn't clear on the vision for the company and is looking to the Leadership Team to either provide it or help make it clear in the CEO's own head. Recipe for failure. Every single time.

The Leadership Team

As I see it, the purpose of the Leadership Team is to take the vision for the company the CEO provides, clearly understand their individual accountabilities in bringing that vision to life, break it into smaller, bite-sized pieces across each leader's department, set expectations and timelines for their direct reports, and sit back and watch the magic happen with occasional course corrects along the way. Hopefully, they've hired, trained, and empowered managers who will then take that information and do the same thing for their direct reports and so on, all the way down the chain.

However, what I've seen happen in the most recent companies I've worked is the CEO's vision is weak or not clearly stated enough so leaders create their own versions of that vision based on what they perceive the CEO means (but couldn't clearly articulate) with a healthy dose of, "Well, when I worked at Company X this is what worked best for me," attached to the message traveling down the chain. Add to it the same, self-aggrandizing behaviors with each descending level of management and you end up with a vision that has been iterated so far away from its original state that no one even knows what the original vision was. This leads to confusion in the lower ranks and increasing levels of frustration higher and higher up the chain.

Again, if the message emanating from the Big Cheese isn't crystal clear it is officially open to interpretation. And that interpretation travels leader-to-leader down to the most junior employee in the company and back up the chain as some version that no one is familiar with. It's important to spend the time, however long it takes, to make sure that messaging is crystal clear at the very top level before messaging down the chain. Or the shit show that ensues will not only be annoying as fuck, but will result in wasted time and money, annoyed and burnt-out employees, and the all-too-familiar levels of attrition and ship-to-ship jumping implicit with early-stage companies that don't have their shit together. If you're an established company still experiencing issues such as this, you're essentially hopeless and truly need to rethink the leadership in your organization. Yep, I said it.

CEO or Buddy? Choose Well.

Something I've noticed with younger and newer CEOs is that they want to be portrayed as approachable. They shirk the glass tower that heritage CEOs have coveted for decades and do their best to fund (and attend) the company beer bashes, sit out among the team vs. in an enclosed office, and be as present and visible as possible as to not appear elitist or above it all. This practice is extremely effective in startups and early-stage companies but is borderline impossible to maintain once a company is 100+ employees deep and when a CEO's time is not only more expensive but better spent creating cohesion among their Leadership Team and ideating on the next iteration of the company or product.

In my years as a career, C-suite Executive Assistant I've mastered creating visibility for my bosses in the eyes of their employees. I've known exactly when to insert them into company-wide activities, when to message the company about crunchy topics and exactly how to do it, and when to put their asses back in the ivory tower with strict orders to "zip it" until I and the rest of the Leadership Team can get a handle on flagging morale, a high-visibility exit or termination, or a change of course instituted by my CEO that may not have gone as planned and caused flames of dissent in the ranks where once there was only a flicker.

CEOs have an ever-changing fine line to walk as the company grows in headcount. It's important for newer CEOs to understand that everyone will not look at them as a peer. Like, ever. They will always be the Big Cheese in their employees' eyes and someone who will always elicit a bit of fear with their presence, even when swigging an IPA alongside them at the company happy hour while talking about the latest NBA trade. That is immense power and rather conspicuous hierarchy that most newbie CEOs can't quite comprehend, especially if they were once a rank-and-file member of a company before becoming CEO overnight. It's important to understand that everything changes once those three letters get appended to the end of your name. Sure, leaders can be friendly, but can no longer be friends. At least, not demonstratively out in the open, for fear of claims of favoritism or nepotism. Sure, they can be present, but not too present, for fear of employees confusing their openness and approachability for full, unfettered access at any point in time. Sure, they can be a "bud," but at some point, the person they're buds with may underperform dramatically, forcing them to have to issue a termination edict that's personally painful and having a noticeable effect on company morale.

As a leader, that line between authoritarian and buddy is one that's not only difficult navigate but just as difficult to enforce. Don't do it alone. You have an incredible resource sitting right outside your door or within arm's reach in the form of your Executive Assistant, and if you're hip to the game, your Chief of Staff/Executive Assistant team. Empower them correctly and you will have a PR team who will help you navigate deftly through the tricky waters of friendliness and approachability in your growing organization while keeping you just far enough above the line-of-fire that takes many CEOs out.

The New CEO Dream Team: Chief of Staff and Executive Assistant

Many CEOs are finally getting hip to the game. They're realizing that at a certain point in their company's maturation they need a certain level of assistance and guidance that can't come solely from their Leadership Team. In fact, they often need help wrangling their own Leadership Team and making sure that their vision isn't being diluted when communicated down and back up the chain of command. That's where a dope-ass Chief of Staff and Executive Assistant team becomes essential.

The Chief of Staff is, essentially, a mini-me of the CEO. An empowered Chief of Staff becomes equal parts enforcer and executioner (at times) for the CEO and ensures that messaging and accountabilities are clear, timelines are established and consistently met, team members have everything they need from the CEO to execute effectively, and can start cracking skulls if shit goes awry, with the full support of the CEO. In short, it's about the shittiest job one could ever aspire to because they are essentially seen as the biggest asshole in the company to both the Leadership Team and all of their direct reports all the way down the chain. The role is purely about results. That's it. It's a role with immense pressure, tons of autonomy and accountability, and based on creating and maintaining operational and administrative efficiency up and down the chain of command. This role is often looked at as accessory and not critical to the success of the company. I couldn't disagree more. In fact, it's been proven in numerous, ubiquitous organizations in the wild, that adding this additional layer of support tremendously improves the efficiency and effectiveness of the C-suite and Leadership

Team, and exponentially decreases overall company attrition.

A Chief of Staff typically becomes the direct supervisor of the CEO's Executive Assistant, who is the administrative Wonder Twin to the Chief of Staff. Together, they become the operational and administrative nerve center for the company and allow the CEO to focus much more consistently and effectively on higher-level responsibilities like fundraising, new products, or building external relationships that drive business and, resultantly, profits.

Often Leadership Teams will look at this additional layer as a hindrance to the uninhibited access to the CEO they've become accustomed to. And, yes, there is often pushback, hazing, and all of the typical, regressive behaviors ex-Ivy League frat boys with fragile egos engage in anytime they feel their autonomy or power is threatened. However, if given an opportunity to flourish and succeed and with a bit of lean in by the Leadership Team, the addition of the Chief of Staff/EA to CEO partnership can make everyone in the C-suite exponentially more effective with much of the more granular, time-consuming, productivity management and PR handled by the new dream team. This allows for more effective face time between CEO and Leadership Team and with the Leadership Team and their direct reports. Get into it. It's a thing now.

Chapter Two:
Company Culture

The Company Culture Myth

As someone who's been a worker for most of my career supporting CEOs and leaders in numerous industries let me just say this, in no uncertain terms:

You have little-to-no control over company culture.

Company culture is created by the people who work at the company. Not a bunch of clueless, under-socialized, White dudes sitting in a big, fancy room once a week trying to apply yet another failed theory on company culture that Bezos, Elon, Gates or Dorsey tried at their companies that kind of worked for them. Let me be really clear, here. You cannot create your company's culture. You can set parameters within which it can manifest. That's it. No magic bullet. No perfect blueprint. No copy-and-paste from another company's perceived success at it.

Dear HR/People Team:

Please STFU with your theories about creating company culture. We both know it's not physically possible. The gig is up. In fact, you're part of the problem. In your efforts to create company culture you actually homogenize it to the point where it really doesn't work. You hire the same people you hired yesterday and create this weird-ass template that you apply to all candidates who walk through the door. You assume these "birds of the same feather flock together" attitudes and fill the company with middling employees with compliant-enough attitudes and predictable-enough personalities, thereby robbing companies of that handful of mavericks who will, indeed, ruffle a few feathers, shake shit up, challenge established norms and ideals and, yes, push a few people to the edges of their own sanity. But those are "the crazy ones, the misfits, the rebels, the troublemakers, the round pegs in the square holes..." that Steve Jobs talked about who actually change the world, or at the very least, make companies better.

The HR Conundrum

The current state of the Human Resources department and the role itself is a joke. Yeah, I said it. It's a can't-win proposition. C-suites enlist HR specialists to create an open and inclusive company culture yet set these impossible standards and hiring parameters within which they are forced to navigate. HR must then delude employees into thinking that they are on their side and can provide a safe space to air their grievances, advocate on their behalf, and actually hear them when they come through the door crying about today's transgression, pointing out obvious inequities, or making suggestions that could actually help improve company culture. Unfortunately, HR reps are actually beholden to the execs who sign their paychecks and must act in the company's best interests over those of the employee. Which, automatically, sets them up for failure.

Over the years, people have gotten hip to the HR game and avoid the department like the plague. They've likely been screwed over one too many times and would rather take the abuse or ignore the atom bomb falling from the sky just to avoid being fucked over yet again by their friends in HR. If you're in HR, I apologize. Not for what I think about your chosen career path. More to you, personally, knowing that you were dealt a pretty shitty hand just by joining the ranks of HR in today's business climate.

Companies need to be transparent about the function of HR

As I see it, today's HR has an identity problem. HR originally began as an administrative-oriented, process-driven role. It was there to serve a singular purpose: Get employees set up with everything they need, administratively, then sit back and watch it all come together, with a light tug on the reins from time-to-time to course correct. Yes, step in and refer rogue employees back to the rather lengthy employee manual that clearly outlines the expectations and rules of engagement of being an employee at the company, but not much more than that. Somewhere between then and now HR has taken on the role of armchair psychologist, legal arbitrator, and culture czar. All without specific degrees and rigorous training in each of those modalities. Big mistake. HUGE!

By relegating HR as the Benedict Arnold of the company, they're immediately seen as untrustworthy by the very employees they're tasked to serve. Any complaint someone logs with HR, we all know, will eventually end up in a hastily crafted email that lands with a big, fat thud in the CEO's inbox. Worse is the complaint will likely be lacking the same amount of context, emotion, and clarity with which it was delivered, and tinged with a bit of bias toward the company vs. the employee. The ultimate goal of HR is to protect the company's interests, placate a stressed employee, talk them off the ledge, or find a legal way to terminate them or the situation to avoid spoiling the all-too-important company culture they've attempted (and failed) to create. Just like I believe parents can't be their children's best friend and still yank the reins effectively, I believe the same thing of HR. Simply put, they're doing too much. And it's now created a department that every employee in business these days is wary of and avoids at all costs which is completely antithetical to the resource part of the HR title.

Many startups hold out until the very last moment to hire HR professionals because they truly don't understand the intrinsic value a strong HR team can provide a company. While I disparage HR in general, when administered and empowered correctly, they truly do provide the type of bilateral support that helps a company scale effectively while keeping the company's train cars securely planted on the tracks. Unfortunately, the reality is that they are typically seen by employees as underpowered, less-than-covert agents of the C-suite, who will always side with the company no matter how valid the complaint may be. As a result, most want nothing to do with HR, often, including the C-suite they're designed to support.

Perks or Shackles?

Can we please cut the bullshit re: offering employee perks as a tool for building culture? This is one of the most annoying untruths I see and have experienced firsthand. In fact, I'm guilty as hell for jumping on the bandwagon myself.

Perks like free food, unlimited vacation, in-office coffee shops, and happy hours serve one real purpose: keeping butts in seats longer. There you go. Myth busted. You're welcome.

Offering free food allows an employee to simply get up from his desk, walk a few feet or to another floor and grab anything their taste buds desire. That choreography usually takes far less than the hour allotted employees, by law, for a lunch break. Sure, sell it as a convenience or a perk all you want. That employee, of course, will appreciate the convenience and partake, pretty much, every day thinking that their company is the greatest in the history of ever. But, over time, several deleterious things occur.

The Startup 15

Ask any employee at any super sweet startup or early stage company that offers free food and they will giggle in agreement. Startup employees at perk-laden companies typically gain 10-15 pounds over time because food is so plentiful and within a short walk that only the most self-aware, stringent dieters can resist that extra helping or the daily, freshly baked cookies or the superfluous chips and sodas on offer. For a workforce that's mostly in their 20s and 30s, this company-sponsored obesity is a reality. Having that sort of access to food leads to overeating, stress eating, and consuming insane amounts of carbohydrates while sitting or standing in one place for 10 to 12 hours per day, with only those short breaks and short jaunts for free food. It creates terrible eating habits. And companies are complicit. Sure, you could make the argument that people need to be accountable for their own health and have self-control. Keep putting a chocolate cake in front of a kid every day and see how it takes before he cracks and nom nom's the fuck out of that cake that day and every day thereafter. Companies are setting employees up for failure with the free food bonanza. It's literally placing kids in a candy store and expecting them to take one small piece. Ain't gonna happen.

"Startup Disease"

Also known as severe Vitamin D deficiency. My doctor pointed this out to me once during an annual check-up. I clearly remember watching him stare at my chart, furrowing his brow, and asking me what I do for work. At the time I was working at Square, officially still a startup at the time. He shook his head in disdain and said, "You've got startup disease." He explained that almost all of his patients who worked at startups have abysmally low levels of Vitamin D, mainly caused by not going outside for lunch or breaks to get natural sunlight. I thought about it for all of about a minute and realized that in that entire month I had only been outside while walking from the train to work and vice versa. And because of daylight savings time, it was dark out both times. Since the company was offering three squares a day, had a full-on coffee shop on site, and even had beer taps and happy hours almost every day there was really no reason to leave the office. In fact, my appointment that day was the first time I'd actually had natural sunlight during the workweek that entire month. It was rather eye-opening for me and I always made an effort to get out of the office once a day while the sun was shining. It also allowed me to give my company a little side-eye re: all the perks acting as an electric fence for their flock. Keeping employees within the building meant that they would likely grab something quickly and get right back to work, several times throughout the day. A win for the company re: productivity. But literally creating a health hazard for the employees with a dangerous deficiency that could lead to a host of other health issues. But health insurance is free too, so, there's that.

Unlimited Vacation and Sick Leave

Straight-up bullshit. Yeah, I said it. There's an unwritten rule that you never take two or three consecutive weeks of vacation without expecting to lose your job shortly after you return. And "sick" means that something is conspicuously falling off your body or you are verifiably hospitalized. And even then, there's pressure to check-in via cell phone with a quick selfie right before they wheel you into surgery.

The most annoying thing ever is employees coming to work with the flu and spreading that shit department to department because they simply want to appear like they are a trooper and in it to win it. The only thing it achieves is a rolling wave of illness that, inevitably, kills a company's productivity numbers for months until, essentially, everyone has caught it and gotten over it. Again, this starts at the top. CEOs walking into the building hacking and coughing and sitting in meetings setting the example and expectation filters down to the most junior employee in the building. No one wants to appear as weak to their peers and especially to their managers, who are just as guilty of the practice. This needs to stop. Especially as flu strains appear to be gaining in strength beyond the flu shots aimed at defeating them.

According to the Centers for Disease Control, between 20.4 - 23.6 million people contracted the flu during the period of October 1, 2018 and

February 23, 2019. Of that number 252,000 - 302,000 people were hospitalized. And, sadly, of that number 16,400 - 26,700 people died. The flu shot over the past two years is proving only 40% effective against the most recent, more powerful strains of the flu. Now, let's factor in the number of flu-sick employees showing up at the office, touching the same door handles, faucets, dishes, remotes, etc. likely not washing their hands on a regular basis and, essentially, ensuring the company of an epidemic. Again, the move should be to insist that sick employees stay the fuck home. If they want to work while they're there, fine. That's on them. But at least they're confining their contagion to the walls they inhabit and not unleashing it on an entire company of innocent victims. I'm sure that free food is one of the reasons they rally. I say allow them to expense Uber Eats and stay the hell away.

Now, let's talk about this unlimited vacation nonsense. On paper this sounds like the most awesome thing ever. It's adulting to the max! But be not fooled by that shiny little word "unlimited." There are implicit limits on said unlimited vacation.

Dot com 1.0 ushered in the whole work hard/play hard culture that we are all now victim to. Somehow, vacation time got roped into this nonsense. Instead of taking a nice, long, highly curated vacation for a couple of weeks, we got pressured into taking no more than about three days at a time. To most people of this generation, it literally feels unfathomable to take a 3-week vacation without anxiety worthy of a heart attack. It just ain't happenin'. In fact, two weeks would only be an option if you're a rockstar at the company, have worked there for at least a couple of years, and have elicited some modicum of worry from your boss that you might be close to burnout or burning the building down. Then it's okay. But only then. Competent employees who actually use their supposed unlimited vacation to take week-long getaways numerous times per year are low-key first in line to get terminated if any sort of departmental downsizing is proposed. I've seen it happen more times than I care to count.

Unlimited vacation is the Sirens' Song. It lures the unsuspecting candidate to sign their promise-laden offer letter, cash their juicy sign-on bonus check, and sit in their comfy Aeron chair facing their gleaming new 27" Apple monitor and peel the protective film themselves off their sweet new Space Grey Apple laptop. You know, the one they'll use to book the flights to Fiji in a few months to take advantage of some of that unlimited vacation. Dead man walking.

Again, this culture was created and is exemplified at the top level. CEOs who consistently work 12-hour days, rarely see their children, send company-wide emails at all hours of the evening, and never take actual vacation set the tone for the entire company. Think about it. If the CEO doesn't do it, what gives an employee the license to do it without some form of low-key disdain or side-eye from their managers who are only following the lead set by the CEO? This behavior has a trickle-down effect throughout the organization and, historically, the lower the manager the more ridiculous and pervasive this practice becomes. Lower-level managers are intent on climbing the ladder so they're going to mirror, 3x, the actions and habits of their manager, who has mirrored, 2x, the actions and habits of their manager, and so on up the chain. Which means that taking vacation is seen as a form of weakness or lack of dedication by anyone who doesn't mirror the actions and habits of the person they report to. Obviously, this leads to employee burnout, flagging company morale, and a company culture that's more sweatshop than the bright, shiny, collaborative, ping pong-laden culture that was sold to employees ad nauseam during their interview cycles.

People need a physical and emotional break from work. Google that shit. There's scientific proof everywhere on the Internet that employees are happiest when they can have time to completely unplug from their day-to-day work responsibilities, experience new energy, scenery, and cultures that allow all of their synapses to fire again, and return to work with a refreshed mind that's likely more excited and creative than when they left.

Fuck your unlimited vacation unless you actually mean it. It's a cruel little carrot dangled in front of an unsuspecting, prospective employee that you then snatch away and replace with invisible shackles. It creates burnout and distrust and promotes a culture of work-until-you-drop, and then we'll come to your rescue and insist that you take some time off. What a bunch of bullshit. I say we go back to the whole 2-3 weeks of vacation dynamic and make sure that managers at every level know that it's an employee's right to take it in whatever way they see fit. Same with sick time. Companies should allow sick employees the opportunity to work from home and video in if they're ill and not dare bring their plague into the office. Yet another reason I'm a huge advocate for working remotely on a regular basis and flipping the physical office concept on its head. So many of these issues could be resolved by getting on board with working remotely. We already do it for crying out loud. Check the time stamps on those emails before you go to bed.

Work/Life Balance

Okay, let's nip this shit in the bud, right now. There is no, true, work/life balance. It doesn't exist, people. The phrase du jour is work/life integration. (Thanks, Jeff Bezos.) In today's work environment, it's nearly impossible to find a balance between work and your personal life without some sort of overlap. Sure, you can strike some semblance of balance, but I'd wager an appendage that it's nothing with any true consistency. Sadly, work is just that pervasive in our lives these days because we've allowed it to be, to the point where its integration is an expectation.

By allowing for work/life integration we're acknowledging that work has become an integral part of our lives and even part of our identity. It's what we're judged on most. It's what results in us being able to pay our kids' tuition, purchase that house in the good neighborhood, and afford those fancy vacations we often never take. For a majority of us, work has become who we are, whether or not we care to admit it. The only way to escape this phenomenon is to become independently wealthy and eliminate working within someone else's rules as an obligation. Otherwise, we're stuck with including work in some capacity in our day-to-day lives that are likely centered around our hours at the office.

Onsite Mental Health Professionals

I find it annoyingly ironic that companies offer free food so that employees can be more productive, happy hours and culture-building events so that employees end up becoming other employees' best friends because they, essentially, live at the office, yet they offer no onsite mental health services to help employees deal with the stresses of the consistent 10+ hour workdays, the lack of weekday sunshine they take in, the loneliness from losing friends and relationships from work-induced lack of socialization, the weight gain from all the free food and drinks, and the blue meanies that often creep up when employees feel like they're living to work vs. working to live.

In case you've been living under a rock, there is a global, mental health epidemic that is getting worse by the year. We've all seen the recent spike in high-profile suicides in the news. And that's not including the thousands of work-related suicides per year that don't make headlines. I'm confident in saying that companies are complicit. Though their intentions may appear good on paper, companies are creating a toxic culture that is based more on the work produced by an employee than keeping the employee whole, physically and emotionally, so that they can be both productive and healthy.

We really need to augment this every-perk-in-the-book office culture by adding onsite mental health services to the amenities list. And NO, this should not be HR. They are neither mental health professionals nor psychologists. There should be dedicated, highly qualified, mental health advisors onsite, every day, so that someone who is struggling in silence can pop by for some quick coaching or get some help dealing with a problem either at work or in their personal lives that could be negatively affecting their performance. I believe that if a service like this were available to me at many of the companies where I previously worked, I likely would never have left.

As humans, our primary motivation is validation. Businesses unfairly task people managers, with little-to-no actual management experience, with not only getting the best work out of their teams on a consistent basis, but also making sure they are "okay" and course-correcting them empathetically when their productivity starts flagging. Obviously, more often than not, this doesn't happen. Instead, you have managers with no experience who are trying to learn as they go, resorting to methods used by their favorite, previous managers as a guideline, and throwing everything at the wall to see what sticks. Add in deadlines, accountabilities, and ego and you end up with very little actual management being achieved. Instead, you have managers using FITFO (figure it the fuck out) as a management tool and leaving employees to fend for themselves emotionally.

Having onsite emotional support is a way for companies to take a massive, unspoken, burden off of the management layer and allow employees the me-centric, validation they often need in-the-moment. Sometimes just having someone's undivided attention, who will listen attentively, and offer a much needed, compassionate word or two is really all an employee needs to feel like they're heard, they matter, and they're "not crazy." I've counseled scores of employees throughout the years and know this to be true.

If you must keep your "sweetest place to work in the history of ever" culture and perks plans, prioritize making onsite mental health services part of that plan. And no, mental health services as part of an employee's health care plan isn't what I'm talking about. This is a point-and-click world now. There needs to be someone, somewhere within the office, where employees can either pop by for 15 minutes, or schedule time during the day. What you'll find is that, depending on the size of your company, you'll need more than one. These people should be completely independent of HR as well but, of course, escalate (as independent professionals) anything that is way over the line or could be deemed dangerous or injurious to that specific employee or to other employees within the company. Then, and only then, should HR be brought into the loop.

Chapter Three:
The Worker

Worker Mentality

What defines a great employee now? What qualities? What results?

We join companies with the best of intentions, feeling empowered and ready to assert ourselves for the benefit of our managers, the company, and yes, to feed our own egos a bit with each win we're recognized for. The reality, we find, is we've joined companies often with under-baked managers who are spending more time mitigating the perception that they have no clue what they fuck they're doing vs. actually managing their teams.

We're surrounded by employees who, like us, joined the company with the same, great intentions only to end up feeling surly, unchallenged and defeated. Still, they show up every day to collect the check. I've witnessed many a slow death of overachievers who were aggressively poached from other companies to come and set fire to stagnation on a team only to discover that the manager was the problem causing the team to phone it in every day praying that someone in upper management would get a clue, replace the manager hopefully with one of them. However, in most of the engineering-biased startups I've worked, these conversations never occurred. People would become more and more frustrated, make up narratives of their own about the C-suite not caring, and emotionally check out, do just enough work to keep their heads above water and collect the check, enjoy all of the free shit offered by the company, and quit once a better situation presented itself.

One thing I hammer home in my workshops is personal accountability. It's important to understand that your individual contribution to a company is based primarily on how you show up each day. Your attitude is a key contributor to your success, even if conditions at the company aren't ideal or as you'd hoped after you signed your offer letter. Sure, there are situations and work environments that simply suck, be they too hierarchical, poorly managed, nepotistic, etc. Those are the situations you extricate yourself from ASAP. However, as a coach, I continue to endure endless whining and complaining about companies and managers by employees who have completely exonerated themselves from blame for why they perceive their company is going to shit. Sorry. Not buying it.

Employees, generally, have handed over the reins a bit too willingly. Many show up with what I call *worker mentality*, a "what's in it for me" attitude that relieves them of any responsibility for the health and prosperity of the team they're on aside from their individual contribution. Over time they become disenfranchised when their ideas aren't advanced instead of continuing to fight for what they know is right or could help the team succeed. They sit silently, brooding away in meetings and return to their desks to send a handful of surly Slacks about how stupid the meeting was without taking into account they had every opportunity to raise their hand and be heard.

My grandmother used to tell me, "One monkey don't stop the show." And I believed her. I showed up every day with the same, clear goal: Make an impact. No rogue employee or bad manager could ever stop me from achieving that objective because it was solely mine. The impact that I chose to make, even in small increments, was purely up to me. Fighting for an initiative and continually re-crafting my message until it was accepted and adopted was part of how I showed up as a passionate, slightly aggressive employee every day. Yes, I ruffled feathers, but never with the intent to do so. I simply wanted my voice to be heard and given a fair shake and opportunity to make an impact.

For instance, anytime a manager rejected one of my ideas I didn't get salty face, fold my arms and immediately stomp to the water cooler to express my disdain for the company with the other crows gathered 'round doing the same. I would assess whether or not my message was clear or relevant enough. I asked clarifying questions to understand the "no." I'd try to understand the opposing viewpoint, in detail, so that I could figure out what the blockers were, specifically, to vet whether they were factual or emotionally-based. From there I would craft a strategy intent on changing their mind. If I still couldn't get through and my idea still got rejected, I'd already done enough research to ascertain whether or not I was dealing with someone rational or emotional. If my ideas were too often rejected without facts, then I knew I either had to circumvent that particular manager or consider leaving the company if that manager was the CEO.

I've never subscribed to worker mentality. That's likely because I've been both worker and small business owner several times throughout my professional career. What I've learned as a worker directly influenced how I ran my businesses. And what I learned as a business owner directly influenced how I showed up as a worker.

As a worker, it's imperative to be acutely aware that you have an important responsibility as an employee. That is, to show up every day and do your very best work, regardless of circumstance, be hyper prepared, express opinions based in fact not emotion, and contribute your ass off with a great attitude, a strong work ethic, while reliably meeting or exceeding expectations. Kinda simple, really. It's when we fall victim to worker mentality, believing we don't have the respect we deserve, can't make an impact because we're cockblocked relentlessly, or becoming convinced that our managers are idiots and are somehow out to make our lives completely suck, that we become those crows at the water cooler blithely exonerating themselves from any responsibility and looking for external validation that should be supplied, in abundance, internally.

Business has changed. The rules have changed. Now, more than at any time in the history of business employees have the opportunity to be heard and make an impact. Leadership Teams are much more open to opinions, feedback and ideas than in decades past because leaders now understand that some of the best ideas come from the most unlikely sources. However, employees still fear that knock on the CEO's door. They let great ideas get dusty or even die for fear of rejection or ridicule. I've always held that an idea, even if rejected, leaves a subconscious footprint. It plants in the mind of the listener that you were passionate enough to share it and often leads to another idea or discussion based on your original idea. This creates positive momentum and could actually score you a mention at the company all-hands meeting or even a co-creator listing on a patent because you made the effort to leave that subconscious footprint in the first place.

Back to Basics

As we rise through the ranks as workers, we often fall victim to the work vs. the mission. Instead of seeing the entire forest, our focus often turns to the tree directly in front of us. As a result, we lose awareness of the vision of the company and the passion laid out by the most important person in the company: the CEO.

I like to do an exercise anytime I'm stressed out by deadlines or consistently muttering, "Man, fuck this place," as I bemoan the fact that I'm working somewhere or for an executive I simply cannot stand. That exercise is to root through the myriad of emails on my personal email account, locate and re-read those emails during my interview cycle that made me jazzed enough about the company to make the decision to join. I try to put myself back in that headspace to see if I can recreate that feeling and remember some valuable tidbit or emotion that snaps me out of my displaced anger and back into the wide-eyed, biggest fan who walked through the door on day one.

Part of this exercise is to extricate myself from my own pity party and try to insert myself into the shoes of my boss, typically the CEO. What was his vision? How did he pull it all together? What was he hoping to achieve when he started the company? What must he be going through? What sacrifices did he make to bring this vision to fruition?

Often, we forget that there is a human being on the subject end of the CEO title. There's someone, a lot like us, who likely had a really cool idea while in the shower one morning, ran it past a couple of trusted friends, did some sound research, decided to side hustle the idea, eventually quit his job, and give it a go. Or daddy cut him a check, he called three buddies from his frat, rented a WeWork, and joined the ubiquitous bro-hood called a "startup."

As workers we're so consumed by the minutiae that we completely miss out on the journey and the mission, the two most important parts of the maturation of a company. As I see it, if we focused on those components more than the perks being offered, the hours being worked, and the salary we're hoping to score, we would be much less unhappy in our roles and could simply refer back to the why to help recalibrate our attitudes.

Today's Successful Worker

I've read so many books written about successful CEOs. The secrets of becoming one. The personality traits of the most successful ones. Rags-to-riches stories. You name it! But what beguiles me is the fact that no one has written a book about what it takes to be a successful worker. Not everyone wants to be a CEO. Not everyone has the aptitude, personality, or chutzpah to be one. Some people are perfectly content showing up to work every day, dealing with whatever situation they're dealt, hopefully making an impact and having a voice, collecting a respectable paycheck, and heading home to be with their friends and loved ones and spend quality time. For some, work is a necessary evil. And there is absolutely nothing wrong with that.

Dot-com 1.0 created this expectation of work hard/play hard and ushered in today's new normal and misperception that work is everything. Crushing it. Being number one. Success at all costs. It doesn't take an Einstein to see what toll that's taken on our society. Burnout is so common it's now considered a weakness instead of the mental and physiological medical condition it is. I'd honestly say that obsession with work has contributed heavily to the failed marriages and broken homes we constantly hear about or have personally experienced. It has definitely created a mental health epidemic that was only recently directly associated with this work hard/play hard mentality.

I'm guilty. I've been hospitalized twice with what were thought to be heart attacks from stress and hypertension. I grew up professionally during dot-com 1.0 and worked in Investment Banking for most of it. While I admit I did kind of enjoy the insane pace, freneticism, volatility, and hedonism of the time it twice almost cost me my life, once at 27 and again at 31. My ambition was stoked by the wild successes of the bankers around me, the fancy parties, the fat bonus checks, the parade of new BMWs driven by analysts only a year out of college. The expectations had risen so high that in order to be taken seriously, even as an Executive Assistant, a Black, gay, male one at that, you had to perform at a level that was borderline superhuman. And I did. Almost to my demise.

Luckily, it feels we've backed off the accelerator a bit during dot-com 2.0. Sure, there is still immense pressure to perform, but it's less extreme. Which, ironically, makes it even more dangerous.

Showing Up

Here's a thought. Since we spend, on average, 9 - 11 hours at work each day, why not really show up? One of the most annoying things about my work experiences is having to endure people who are not as passionate about their jobs as I am. When I join a company, I tend to be the biggest cheerleader in the building. I've done my due diligence. I've vetted the passion of the CEO and their Leadership Team. I've learned the products and mastered all of the acronyms. I understand and follow our competitors' moves. And I'm ready, each day, to use my entire toolbox of skills, experience, connections, and abilities to help my company and my bosses succeed. And then you run into that one or two employees who just don't give a flying fuck. They're bitter, slow to react, and often toxic on a level that defies comprehension. Somehow, they've managed to stay employed by the company and are waging their own secret war to make everyone's lives pure hell until they get fired, severanced, or hit by a bus.

Being a successful worker by today's standards requires a complete shift in the traditional mindset. Gone are the days of the easy 9-to-5. Managers are so busy trying to hit their KPIs that they don't have (or make) time to spend on each of their direct reports' professional development. Which means that's now left to the employee to figure out for themselves. And, personally, I think that's a great thing.

So, how can you become a great employee in today's business paradigm?

1. Show up! Stop just collecting the check and show up with the intent of making an impact every day. And that impact has to be initiated and managed by you. It can't be dependent on the whims or actions of others. You determine the impact you want to make, big or small, and focus on achieving that objective. If you get blocked, go around. If you get blocked relentlessly and run out of go around options, book an appointment for a fantastic manicure, come back and flash both perfectly manicured middle fingers and go find a situation or team who will appreciate and welcome your contributions. Remember: "One monkey don't stop the show."

2. Contribute or shut the fuck up. If you don't contribute to conversations or assert your vetted opinions when the opportunities present themselves, that's on you. It's no one's fault but yours. And please spare me the whole shyness argument. I'm sorry, it's bullshit. Part of showing up in business is sticking your neck outside the shell from time-to-time without fear of rejection or perceived ridicule. Do this enough times and you'll never battle with confidence again. But you've got to build the muscle. Nothing frustrates me more than watching an employee with great ideas willingly choose not to share them in an open forum. Worse, is when they then head to the water cooler to complain to the other crows about the managers in the room who seem to be so unconcerned about their employees' opinions. You know what? Get out. Just go. Seriously. If you can't advocate for yourself and choose not to voice your opinions or contribute to the conversation, then you officially relinquish your right to complain. Period.

3. Stop caring. We care too much about the opinions of others. We seek way too much external validation which often impedes our ability to simply tell the truth or offer an opposing view. I'm Team DGAF. My truth is not dependent on someone else's validation. I take the time to vet my opinions for fact and deliver them with zero emotion. How someone chooses to take in that information is completely up to them and, frankly, I really don't give a shit beyond that. I know that my intentions are pure, and my opinions are delivered without intentional bias or intent to harm. If they don't like it, cool. Happy to discuss. Doesn't stop the show, however. And, certainly won't deter me from expressing my truth. We've got to get back to telling it like it is without fear or caring about others' perceptions of us when we do. Their opinion of me has yet to cut a check to pay my rent, so...

4. It's about the work. We get so caught up in non-work-related BS like emotions, cliques, water cooler crow cabals, and perceived oppression that we forget why we're even in the building: to do your job and contribute to the success of the company. Focus on just that and you'll quickly uncover numerous opportunities to make an impact and have a voice. Fall victim to worker mentality and you'll continue just collecting the check, annoying the fuck out of the passionate ones, and doing yourself and your professional development a grave disservice, quite publicly, I might add.

5. Step up. Knock on the CEO's door. (Ask the Assistant first or you'll be blacklisted forever). Speak up in meetings instead of meekly observing. Don't suppress your passion to fit in with the crows. F those kids. Do your own research, especially if you don't agree with what's presented. And then present it, without fear. Often what you'll find is that people make mistakes and that extra effort you took could course correct a project and save the company hundreds/thousands/millions of dollars and countless man-hours.

CEO of ME

I'm a huge believer that you should approach your role not as a "worker" but as the CEO of your own small business. This approach allows you to see your role as much more important to your own success first, and integral to the success of the company secondarily. Instead of simply doing a job you are aligning yourself with your #1 client as a top service provider vs. a "worker." This allows you to see your manager as a peer vs. your boss and, at least mentally, levels the playing field.

I've found that by treating my bosses as my #1 clients I feel much more empowered to take calculated risks and be more aggressive and authoritative in my language and actions because, like him, I am a CEO in my own right. My small company and my brand are everything to me and I will do everything in my power to protect my good name. I feel more compelled to get it right the first time, to vet everything thoroughly and thoughtfully, ask the hard questions, and question things I don't necessarily agree with because I don't want my brand attached to anything that doesn't pass muster.

Another benefit to this mindset is the confidence to negotiate on my brand's behalf. One of the things I focus on in my education and strategic workshops is negotiating aggressively on one's behalf. Often Executive Assistants get taken advantage of in the most conspicuous ways. The worst offense is when saddled with additional, high-touch executives to support with little-to-no advance warning and certainly no increase in pay. It's exploitative and wrong.

The Cable Company Approach

As part of being the CEO of ME, I approach the role like a cable company approaches their client relationship. I'll explain:

When you order basic cable, you sign a contract. The cable company dispatches a tech to your home to get you set up with everything you need to provide seamless, uninterrupted service. Everything is great. And then you decide you want to add a sports channel or a movie channel to your basic cable subscription. And, what happens?

The cable company is all too happy to help you upgrade by offering you packages that include everything you're asking for. At a cost. The original contract is voided, and a new contract is created with your additional channels and at a new monthly rate. And you happily pay it, or you will have no service. If the additional channels are too expensive you have every right to stay with your basic cable package or cancel the service altogether and look for another service provider that has everything you want at a rate you want to pay, but likely with poorer reliability and customer service.

Executive Assistants, in this instance, are no different. Executives signed the original contract with the expectation that the EA was going to provide service based on the needs and expectations outlined in that contract. The Executive Assistant set up their own expectations to align accordingly. Then, out of the blue, an exec decides to add another executive to support. The original contract stated one executive to support and suddenly there are two. Which means, essentially, consenting to add another channel to the basic cable subscription, voiding the original contract, and agreeing to a new one at a higher rate. It's quite simple, really. But rarely do I see Executive Assistants stomping on the brakes, dragging their execs back to the table to renegotiate their salaries commensurate with these new accountabilities. Instead, they simply accept the new responsibility without asking for some sort of reciprocity. Would a CEO work for free? Would they allow an exponential increase in their workload without negotiating some sort of remuneration for this new responsibility? Uh, no. Not even for a second.

Having a CEO mentality as a worker benefits you in numerous ways. It allows you to advocate for yourself, quite clearly, in instances like this. It allows you to ignore the office idiots who are trying to distract you from the work and your own professional aspirations. It's Teflon against toxic employees, gossip cabals, and energy vampires who absolutely kill the morale and culture of a company. And it subconsciously makes you less permeable to bullshit, drama, and politics because they don't serve your ultimate goals or intentions.

Communicating What Makes a Good Worker

Something I've noticed is that companies rarely communicate to their employees what they deem to be a good worker or what specific expectations they have of an employee at their company. Often this is buried in the Employee Handbook among lines of legal-eze that completely dilutes the message. And, let's face it, no one in the history of ever really reads that damned Employee Handbook cover-to-cover and only refer to it to confirm the number of vacation or sick days on offer, the outdated org chart, and maybe a passage or two that confirms that the coup they're planning against their sucky manager is, indeed, a terminable offense.

Consistency of messaging is all-too-common when rallying the troops around a project or deadline. So, help me understand why it wouldn't be just important for employees to hear what's expected of them on a consistent basis? Often this could serve as a reminder for legacy employees, benchmarking for newer employees, and firepower for management at every level when having to discipline employees performing or behaving outside of consistently communicated expectations.

Role Leveling

A big issue that I continue to see in the wild is incorrect leveling of roles, specifically in larger companies. I will speak specifically about Executive Assistants since that's the group I know best, though this is a problem at almost every level of the organization.

Leveling should be based on a combination of experience, ability, and accomplishment. Each level should have a set of very specific and easily understood descriptions and requirements to justify an employee being eligible for a certain level. However, what I'm seeing is that these levels aren't clearly defined. They are assumed or represented by some arbitrary or hastily crafted insert in the Employee Handbook likely to quell an uprising within the ranks vs. a thoughtful execution of the requirements to be in each level. This often occurs as a company scales exponentially and quickly and is forced to provide some sort of device to promote overachievers and keep them from heading for the exits.

However, something much more sinister is happening. Because these levels aren't clearly defined and communicated with consistency, managers are cutting corners and promoting those they perceive to be crushing it and who are most visible in their business lives instead of holding everyone to the same, clearly defined, agreed-upon standards that everyone else is. The favoritism is rife and is yet another inequity that many who aren't the most vocal or visible but crushing it just as much as the one scoring the promotion must endure and reconcile.

Within larger companies, Administrative and Executive Assistants often endure the worst of it with regard to incorrect or non-existent leveling, compensation, and the tacit lack of understanding of everything they do. Many high achieving Executive Assistants are passed over for promotions and compensation adjustments, ironically, because they make their executive's lives so easy with their Herculean efforts that executives assume that not much effort went into all that calm water on the surface. Little do they know that Mount Vesuvius is erupting on the regular just under the surface and the battle to create all that calm is insanely intricate and difficult. Worse, is that the "hot chick with a big rack" who's doing an okay job is always given deference in a misogynist-tinged C-suite, while the aging or not-as-hot EA who is absolutely murdering it behind the scenes and likely covering for the lackluster efforts of the "hot chick" has to fight for the recognition, compensation, and respect they deserve in abundance.

This kind of behavior and disrespect has plagued this role for decades. In my 27 years as an EA I've not seen it get much better. In fact, I've seen it get a bit worse. And it's mainly because leveling for Executive Assistants isn't done thoughtfully nor nearly as much by companies with over 1,000 employees. The script needs to be created so that employees have a clearly defined set of requirements to which to align their professional development goals. Without them they are left to the whims of their managers, the opinions of their peers, and all of the underinformed biases that are pervasive and continue plague management levels.

These levels help managers are well. It gives them a well-defined, vetted guideline with which to assess their direct reports, reward above-and-beyond efforts, coach and mentor those who are underperforming or show promise, and cover their own asses when promotions are handed out and someone disagrees or cries foul. Without these clearly defined levels companies are left exposed to a variety of potential discrimination litigation opportunities including ageism, gender bias, racism, lack of accessibility, and nepotism.

Employees aren't stupid. They know what's up. They watch idiots and phonies get promoted ahead of them all the time. They know when a promotion was handed out to someone completely undeserving and often have to battle their own anger and disappointment just to keep from burning the building down. It's incredibly important that companies take the time to flesh out these levels in exacting detail so that everything is above board and completely transparent. Sure, some employees will deserve special consideration when achieving well beyond their years of experience or current level of responsibility, but that should be the exception, not the rule. Unfortunately, companies without clearly defined levels create a Wild West of sorts that manifests in posturing, special favors, favoritism, and all of the BS, high-school behaviors we all lamented while growing up. Yes, Darwinism still exists in the business environment. It should. However, companies need to create an environment where that can happen naturally. Not an environment that promotes its uglier face by avoiding the hard work of leveling roles correctly. This leads to many of the employee morale issues that continue to confound the C-suite and HR/People teams who are more complicit than anyone.

Chapter Four:
Recruiting and Retention

The Recruitment Cycle

Recruiting is one of the most essential functions in business, yet I see it done incredibly poorly more often than not. Job descriptions that read like bad novels. Typos more obvious than a bad toupee. Creative language doing its best to polish a turd job under the guise of "a great opportunity." Please. Most people looking for a job aren't completely dense or apt to fall for such nonsense. Especially if they're applying for 30-50 jobs per day and building an advanced "HR vocabulary" along the way. They can distinguish truth from bullshit in record time and probably tell you the age of the fresh-from-college, hair twirling, HR Generalist who wrote it.

Think about it. Would you actually want to hire some dolt who was hanging on every word of a bullshit-laden job description? What would that person be like as an employee? Would they be objective or wise enough to usurp the nuance in an email chain and alert their manager of an impending catastrophe? Would they (I've seen this) run out and purchase $500 worth of gift cards because a scammer snuck an email through the firewall disguised as the CEO with language that was brief and believable enough to get in his car and head to Walmart to complete the special, secret mission...when the CEO's EA is sitting 4 feet away?

Seriously. Cut the crap, already. Words matter. Everything you present regarding the company, from the jump, will determine the type of employees you attract and potentially add to the team. Be authentic with your words and make sure that the pool from which you're pulling isn't teeming with naive nitwits who just happen to be highly skilled.

Job Descriptions

Why are we still writing lengthy, mostly bullshit, job descriptions in order to attract top talent? We all know that aside from a few essential responsibilities and must-haves, job descriptions are basically worthless as the job is really dependent on the needs in-the-moment and that person's ability to FITFO (figure it the fuck out) based on all their experience vetted by an algorithm and during the interview process. So, I propose we take convention out back, put it out of its misery, and do something a little revolutionary (read: relevant) when seeking top talent.

Let's examine the phrase "top talent." How do you know that you're actually getting someone who's at the top of their game and THE game, especially where it pertains to your specific needs? You're writing the script for them in the job description so you're truly only attracting people who can, at least, read. Yay. But you're leaving an incredible vetting opportunity on the table each time you post a lengthy, mostly irrelevant job description on your exhaustive list of online recruiting websites.

REAL top talent will do the work.

Anytime I've really wanted a particular job and felt like I was the person they needed I've gone completely off-script and written a heartfelt letter or email directly to The Big Cheese, purposely circumventing the whole recruiting process. Just short of stalking in some cases. I wasn't always successful, but the few times that I was turned out to be the best work experiences of my professional career.

Allow the passionate ones to prove themselves from the jump.

The entire recruiting game is rife with ego. The company wants to put its best foot forward with its shiny, beautifully shot videos touting their can't lose product, dopest-in-the-history-of-ever open office design, and culture that eclipses the very best party school fraternities and sororities on the planet. Conversely, top talent knows they are in a hot market and are getting cash and opportunities thrown at them daily resulting in degrees of entitlement and lack of commitment I've not seen since the height of dot com 1.0. But here's the thing. We're now in a standoff. And it's one that could be remedied by putting your money where your mouth is, on both sides.

Here's the job. How would you do it?

Toss your long-ass job description right in that mesh garbage bin over there and flip the script. Instead of writing a long, adjective-laden job description, write it like you would your company's OKRs. Write the top-level objectives and ask the simple question:

How would you construct your role to achieve these objectives?

If you want to immediately weed out 60 - 70% of the chaff who respond to your job postings, give this a try. Most respondents are typically robo-searching job postings and have all but memorized the number of keystrokes it takes to apply for roles, including attaching their resumes. LinkedIn even allows you to apply in one click, completely robbing applicants of any opportunity to differentiate themselves beyond their 2D resumes and saddling internal recruiters with masses of applicants to wade through, most of whom aren't even close to what they're looking for.

Remember essay questions on school exams? I used to love them, because they gave me the opportunity state my case and substantiate my findings, while providing context like problem solving skills, writing ability, and powers of persuasion for the reader. We're, essentially, treating hiring like a Scantron test. Here's the question and several answers to choose from. GO! I believe it's the primary reason why companies have such a difficult time recruiting people who actually want to be in the building vs. those simply looking for their next source of income.

Blow shit up! Stop setting mouse traps.

Make candidates work for it! Stop allowing top talent to cheat off your test. Companies claim they want passionate employees who can hit the ground sprinting. Let candidates prove they're that person.

Let's use hiring a top-notch Executive Assistant as an example. Here's how I'd approach marketing the role.

Client: John Doe

Company: Obtuse Tech and Parallelogram Capital

Role: Executive and Personal Assistant to CEO

Overview of the Exec and Proposed Role:

John is the CEO of two game-changing companies. He wakes at 4:30 am every morning and is typically booked solid until 10 pm each evening. His schedule is often over-packed and changes at moment's notice daily, so no two days are ever the same. He needs more time to spend with his friends and loved ones and silent time each day to ideate at a high level for the benefit of the teams and products at both companies. Yet he still needs energy and focus to be present with the teams and engage with employees at each company. Additionally, he maintains a healthy media presence and often fields these requests at the expense of his own time.

Given your expertise as a top level Executive Assistant we welcome you to do your necessary due diligence on John and both companies and submit a detailed proposal outlining how you would structure the role, the access/equipment/communication cadence you would need, a realistic projection of the number of daily hours required to be successful, what success in this role would look like if what you propose is followed to-the-letter, and what compensation you would consider commensurate with your contribution, including how long it would take you to get up to speed if given the opportunity. We're not looking for a perfect answer here, but we are looking for the perfect person, so take your time. We look forward to hearing from you.

When I get this proposal back, I'm looking for several key components:

1. Passion. If the candidate writes a thoughtful, detailed proposal complete with metrics and something showing me that they actually took the time and effort to do the due diligence and craft something that aligns quite well to my unstated needs, then I'll definitely know that they're a live one. If they send me a whack, poorly drafted, one paragraph proposal filled with buzz phrases like "I create calm from chaos" yet ask for a deep, six-digit salary because "market's hot," I'll crack my knuckles loudly in anticipation of pressing the delete key...with my middle finger.

2. **Creativity.** I want to know how they think. I want to know how they would approach creating the proposal, what they include, how they advocate for themselves, and how many "hmmm's and eyebrow raises they can elicit from me as I read through.

3. Thoughtfulness. I'm looking for someone who not only knows their shit, but who can take a wide-open canvas with minimal info and create a proposal, however hypothetical, that gives me clear insight into their thought processes and their ability to craft a plausible story. If they've taken the time to Google John, Obtuse Tech, and

Parallelogram Capital, thought about how the CEO gets through the day at each company and how much time he could safely allot to both, factor in some time/ways to eat (on-the-go), set a cadence for "going dark" each evening, managing the communication loop between he and his leadership teams at both companies, etc. then I'm likely to be interested in speaking with that person to learn more about them. How much can you truly usurp from a resume except skill level and experience? And aren't you actually starting from zero at the first phone screen instead of having much more context and insight into who they are and how they roll provided by the proposal?

4. Concision. Anyone can write a narrative. Not everyone can be concise and persuasive with their words. I see it in the numerous resumes I'm asked to review. Adjective log jams that tell me absolutely nothing more than the six essential words I'm looking for describing the actual responsibility. People who write with precision, concision, and authority immediately give a glimpse into their day-to-day ability to get shit done. Those who ramble aimlessly or pad communications with worthless adjectives instantly send up a red flag. I can already tell that any meeting they attend will be filled with long, meandering pontifications that will turn a perfectly curt meeting into an epic eye rolling session and a whole lot of annoyed attendees who can't get a word in edgewise.

5. Grow-er or show-er? We are all blessed with a pretty decent bullshit detector. If you read anyone's writing attentively, you'll quickly feel their passion or unearth a load of scrap metal they're trying to pass off as a new Mercedes. I love confident people. (Grow-ers) I don't love arrogant people. (Show-ers) The one place it's easiest to distinguish between the two is in their writing. Nowhere to hide, my friends. You don't have to be the greatest writer in the world to convey passion, confidence and eagerness. You also don't need to be Sherlock Holmes to figure out that someone is full of it, resting on their self-professed greatness, and writing what they perceive you want to hear vs. what's from the heart and wholly based in fact.

As I've suggested above companies need to blow shit up! We have wasted decades using the same flawed, expensive, time consuming recruiting methods and choreography and achieving the same, mediocre, poor ROI results. In fact, they're worse results given this generation's attention/loyalty deficit and Scantron-test recruiting habits yielding employees who really don't want to be there. But you pay well and the food's free, so there's that.

Relying purely on numbers of applicants in the queue is a decades old and extremely flawed practice. Especially if a majority of those resumes in your recruiters' inboxes just want their bills paid by the salary your company is offering up. Instead, offer up an experience that sets the bar for their employment from the jump. YES, you still have to uphold your end of the bargain by recruiting and onboarding them well. But you set up a much more top professional dynamic by engaging the whole cerebellum of the applicants you want vs. only the prefrontal cortex of those who will pitch a fit for having to "write a frickin' proposal" instead of applying with one click. Choose well.

The Phone Screen

This is your company's first impression. The most important opportunity a company has to position itself as the greatest place to work in

the history of EVER. And you blow it.
Consistently.

Please stop handing your first (recruiting) impression to unprepared, fresh out of school, under-socialized "children." I can't tell you how many phone screens I've had where I've completely nope-d a company from consideration because the 21-year old HR generalist on the other side of the conversation was clearly reviewing my resume for the first time, while I was on the phone no less, and showing up six minutes late for the 30-minute phone call that could potentially change the course of my life or the company. I'm not sure when it became cool for recruiters to be late to a first interview, but this shit needs to stop. I'd say 70% of my phone screens happened late during my last recruiting cycle. And I nexted every single one that did. As I see it, if you're late to the very first opportunity to impress me, you're essentially telling me that I'm not a priority, from the jump. Or that you as a company, not just the employee making the call, don't have your shit together enough to be on time for a simple phone call. It would instantly make me wonder what kind of insanity I would be walking into on day one. Stop wasting candidates' time. Give them a pro from the jump.

The Onsite Interview(s)

Scheduling an onsite interview has become far too difficult and time-consuming than it needs to be, on both sides of the coin. In my last few roles I've noticed that the choreography has become far too complex and companies allow candidates far too much leeway with locking in a simple date and time for an interview. As I see it, if a candidate really wants the job, they will move heaven and earth to make the proposed timing work. A company typically has the more difficult task of wrangling schedules of numerous busy executives, taking conference rooms offline, and making the entire process appear seamless and perfectly executed. There really shouldn't be a bunch of back and forth between a serious candidate and the company to successfully confirm a date and time for an interview. Keep in mind, there are, likely, a number of time-challenged Executive Assistants pulling their hair out, playing endless Tetris with their exec's schedules trying to make something work in a calendar that is already borderline psychotic. This is not only an inconvenience, it's expensive.

And one of the tasks I've always despised as an Executive Assistant myself. Provide several options and low-key force the candidate to choose. Or fuck off. Allowing this process to drag on longer than scoring a date on Tinder is recipe for corporate blue balls. Bigger fish to fry. And less time-consuming, expensive ones at that.

Once you've landed timing for the onsite interviews, it's important to rally all the troops and synch on expectations of the candidate's interview cycle. I've often shown up at onsite interviews and found that no one was prepared or, at best, woefully underprepared. I've also witnessed that the exact same questions were asked by every interviewer on the roster. Question: What exactly does that accomplish other than verifying that the candidate's answers are consistent? I'd offer, not much else. It's a tremendous waste of everyone's time and typically leaves a number of critical questions unanswered by the interviewee.

Synching up ahead of time with all interviewers allows you to make sure that everyone is clear on the objective of the interview cycle for every candidate who enters the building. What do they want to learn from the candidate? What relevant, technical skills does the candidate possess? Which scenarios lend context to whom they are both as a person and as an employee and potential manager? What hints about fit should everyone keep an eye out for? This questioning is a huge responsibility for everyone involved and allows each business unit to get the information they need to make an informed decision.

As a candidate, I can't imagine anything more damning for a potential employer than to endure numerous interviewers, over a period of several hours, asking the same set of boring, unimaginative questions expecting a different answer. Second only to an interviewer asking the ages-old, stupid question, "Where do you see yourself in 5 years?" (Um, writing a book about how fucking tired that question is. That's where.)

Another thing: Anytime I'm waiting to be interviewed and I see someone enter the room holding a clean copy of my resume I instantly start getting nervous. And a little annoyed. If someone enters the room either with the marked-up copy from my previous interviewer or a copy of their own with some notes already scribbled on it I get a bit more excited, knowing that they've actually taken the time to read it ahead of time and formulate some questions before entering the room. Almost every time I've witnessed the latter the interviews have gone swimmingly, and I've usually ended up joining the company. Anytime it was the former, I've not taken the job.

I can't believe I'm even having to say this but: be on time. Seriously, people! I realize things are crazy at your 5-year old "startup" because you're so busy. Snaps for you. But if a candidate is making the effort to arrive at an interview 5-10 minutes early and interviewers show up 5-15 minutes late to the very first interview of six scheduled that day, that gives the candidate 10-25 minutes to ponder whether or not they'd actually want to work at your company based on such a shitty first impression. BE ON TIME. Especially for the first interview of the cycle. If timing shifts a bit because some conversations run a little long that's actually less annoying than having to be made to wait around in an unfamiliar environment, enduring the judgmental gazes of employees walking by and low-key sizing you up.

The Interview (for the candidate)

One thing that I do consistently is to show up to an interview about 10-15 minutes early. I make it a point to arrive early enough to chill in the reception area and observe. The goal is to gather as much passive information as I can while I wait for my interview cycle to start. I watch and listen intently to how employees interact with the receptionist. If people are condescending, abrupt, or brusque it's an indication that there may be respect issues for those in lower-level support roles. Always a red flag. I listen to how the receptionist speaks to those calling in. If he or she is anything other than polite, a bit too casual in tone, or a disorganized mess, it's a sign that they likely weren't properly trained and left to their own devices with one of the single most important functions in the business. This reflects more on the management than it does on the employee. I've been a receptionist before so I know the unique requirements of the job and the insane amount of patience you must have when simultaneously dealing with both external callers and internal employees hovering at your desk, especially when they're being disrespectful or condescending. Again, I'm looking for a receptionist who is incredibly polite, has their shit completely together, and is the classiest voice in the building.

Second, I love to eavesdrop on the casual conversations of employees walking by. Often the reception area is located a stone's throw from the elevators. I don't know what it is, but employees tend to drop the best f-bombs, air their hardcore grievances, and loudly exhale their frustration in that little vestibule right in front of the elevators. I've overheard so many juicy conversations by employees along the lines of, "Man, fuck this place!" or "Oh my God if I don't get out of here, I'm going to stab someone in the eye." As a prospective employee, I'm sitting in the reception area enjoying my mental popcorn and taking ravenous mental notes. Typically, if more than two conversations are along the lines of the aforementioned, I've already usurped there's a problem within the company, be it a bad manager, bad department, or even a bad CEO. And depending on what context I can glean from those conversations I've likely already made my mind up about the company.

The Interview (for the company)

I've been fortunate enough to have some great interviews. On time. Engaged interviewers. Great questions. And I've also had interviews where I was offended to the point of cutting the interviewer off mid-sentence, abruptly ending the interview, and walking out the door never to return. And depending on the severity of the ridiculousness, heading straight onto Facebook, Twitter, Glassdoor and any other medium I could find to regale the story and caution prospective employees who might be considering working at that company. Additionally, I would reach out to the company and cc: everybody under the sun to let them know about my poor experience with hopes that the feedback I provided would help them to refine their process and, maybe, offer a bit more training to the 20-something hair twirler who hadn't pre-read my resume and had the nerve to ask me to sell her a fucking pen as a way to disguise her obvious ineptitude.

Interviews are the only time you will have with a candidate to assess skill, experience, potential fit, demeanor, and aptitude. You only have a short amount of time within which to work, so that time should be choreographed to the minute, be super focused, and cut straight-to-the-point. Sure, presenting yourself as the perfect company is a priority, however assessing whether or not you're getting the perfect employee should be the top priority.

There are so many ways to make candidates feel special without breaking the bank. Add their names to your internal digital signage. Supply a bottle of water or some mints, chocolates, etc. the moment they sit in the conference room. Give them something branded with your logo as a parting gift and make sure it's memorable and highly usable, especially if they are a top prospect. Those little niceties go a long way and create those subconscious "pings" that can be the difference between choosing your company over another that actually pays more but made them feel less special and wanted.

Like a book, interviews should have a beginning, middle, and ending. The entire day should be choreographed with the candidate in mind. Often companies take the path of least resistance and choreograph interviews to fit within blocks of interviewer availability instead of really providing a seamless, unhurried experience to the candidate. Candidates notice this and appreciate when they feel as if people made an effort specifically for them. It's all really perception if you think about it. But it's a perception that can determine whether a candidate signs the offer or doesn't.

The Offer

Companies have got to get this right. Luckily, since the job market is doing well (at time of printing) my last two offers went quite well. Sure, I had to negotiate them to death, but the starting points weren't offensive like in previous years.

In a hot market, where there are more jobs available than top candidates, it's important not to ruin the candidate's experience by presenting an offer that's downright revolting in an effort to preserve your bottom line or "get 'em cheap." Sure, the name of the game is to get someone as cheaply as possible, but it shouldn't be your sole objective. If you're confident you've found the perfect candidate, you should put together an offer that is comprehensive, not solely based on financial compensation. Offers that include RSUs, sign-on bonuses, learning and improvement budgets, and all of the perks allotted by the company are the most attractive offers these days and are, pretty much, the starting point for any company trying to attract top talent.

And here's a little trick: Have the CEO present the offer, or a member of the C-suite. There's something really special about being presented an offer by the person whose name is on the masthead. Obviously, if you're working in a mammoth organization this will be less possible. However, having the CEO present the offer to, say, a junior employee, an Executive Assistant, or a candidate you absolutely **must** have can be the best brand play on the planet. Plus, it's not often that a candidate turns down an offer when presented by the CEO of the company. Subconsciously it feels almost rude and, low-key, like career suicide.

Onboarding

The single biggest misstep I've experienced in the wild is companies not properly onboarding their new employees. It should be criminal. You've expended all of this energy recruiting, shifting schedules, making phone calls, reviewing metrics, choreographing onsite interviews, just to blow it all up by pointing to that seat over there and leaving a new employee to their own devices on Day One. As a career, C-suite Executive Assistant I've only had one onboarding experience that blew me away. Square.

Square One

Square's onboarding process is easily the most impressive thing I've ever witnessed as a new employee. Square figuratively starts from "square one" and reserves a conference room for 4 days for all the new hires from that group. And yes, they start people in hiring groups so that they can onboard them properly. We spent three-and-a-half days in that room learning about the company and the mission in granular detail, having numerous department leads pop in and tell us about their departments and accountabilities, reviewed the employee handbook together, filled out all necessary paperwork together and, at the end of day three, were issued our company laptops and sent to our respective departments for the last few hours of the day to start getting acclimated with our new bosses and teams.

The brilliance of such an approach was this:

It built instant camaraderie. Even the shyest person in the room suddenly had a squad of people he/she felt comfortable with and had some connection to. Going forward they would always have their anniversary date in common. And they would instantly have a lunch buddy for a couple of weeks until they made more friends within the org and, naturally, drifted off into new cliques.

It alleviated anxiety in record time. Joining a company instantly fires the same anxiety synapses as your first day at a new school. It's low-key terrifying even if we don't want to admit it. Don't forget, explosive growth companies can feel very isolating and cold to a new employee. Without some form of forced socialization, companies roll the dice with their new employee's happiness, engagement, and whatever abandonment issues from childhood they may be working through with their therapist. Being in a small group of your equally freaked-out peers and having the consistency of knowing you'll see the same group tomorrow getting the same information and experiencing it together calms that anxiety tremendously and palpably.

It allowed the newbies to hit the ground sprinting. By the time I got to the middle of day three, I was raring to go. I had some new friends. I'd chugged the Kool-Aid. I was proudly rockin' my badass Square t-shirt. And I was ready to own my role and become part of the collective Square team.

Square researched, engineered, and implemented an onboarding process that reads 98% of all other onboarding processes for filth. And the final choke-out: The walk with Jack.

The Walk with Jack

I joined Square because I wanted to work for a CEO who was changing the world in some obvious way. When I decided to leave Levi Strauss, I narrowed my search to two CEOs: Elon Musk and Jack Dorsey. I wrote impassioned letters directly to both of them. Never heard a peep from Elon. Jack got back to me in 2 days. And the rest is history.

I've always long admired and harbored a slightly inappropriate crush on Jack Dorsey. (He's not gay. Calm down.) What absolutely made me realize that I'd made the right decision, even taking a $30K per year pay cut for the honor, was the walk with Jack. Jack Dorsey walks everywhere. It's his jam. On our final morning of Square One we all met on the Embarcadero at a statue of Mahatma Gandhi. We took a group photo with Jack and the crew and, together, walked to the office, each of us spending a few minutes with Jack introducing ourselves, asking a few questions and tagging out.

The fact that this was part of the perfectly curated onboarding process was both mind-blowing and a distinct honor. Not many of us can say that we got to take a walk with and chat up a billionaire, concurrent Founder/CEO of two of the most influential companies on the planet, who actually wanted to be there.

Onboarding shouldn't be some sort of privilege. It should be considered a right, extended to anyone who has expended the time, energy, patience, and vulnerability to accept an offer of employment and choose to join an organization. By dropping the ball on the onboarding process you are sending a terrible message and instantly deflating the hopes of a new employee who really wanted to work at your company. And there's a strong chance you could lose that employee almost as quickly as you procured them and have them run to social media to curse your company for filth. Just as you'd (hopefully) choreographed their interview cycle, pay even closer attention and care to the onboarding process to ensure that your new employee hits the ground sprinting with as little anxiety as possible and with a few quick friends to make the transition much easier.

1.0ers vs. 2.0ers

Having worked in tech startups for the majority of my career there's one phenomenon that causes the most damage within startups and early-stage organizations. And that's the inevitable headcount and culture shift between 1.0ers and 2.0ers.

1.0ers are the employees who helped get the company off the ground, typically the first 50 or so employees. 2.0ers are the bright-eyed, bushy-tailed, newbies who come in with fresh ideas, new energy, and a passion that often trumps the 1.0ers' rocking the bigger stock grants. As companies grow out of startup status and more 2.0ers join the ranks, company morale typically takes a hit. 1.0ers feel less and less special and appreciated because the 2.0ers now dominate the news and hog the perceived spotlight. What sucks is this isn't even a conscious or deliberate practice by management or the C-suite. And therein lies the problem.

Often managers and the C-suite forget the numerous sacrifices that 1.0ers have made in order to help the company grow from Seed Round to a Series A or B funded company. Months, often years of long hours, missed birthday parties, concerts with friends, broken relationships, etc. were a 1.0er's reality during those times. To watch a 2.0er come waltzing through the door and cozily settle into an environment created by a 1.0er and become the new Golden Child is often a really bitter pill to swallow and can often lead to the misperception that the 1.0er has lost their luster and value as an employee. While that may not be wholly true, it often creates bitterness and tension within the team and often leads to the 1.0er being deemed no longer a team player.

I've often counseled 1.0ers on my boss' behalf because they were frustrated with being back-burnered. Funny thing is they really only need a little time and attention paid to them. It wasn't about money or more frequent 1-on-1s. They really only wanted some sort of confirmation that they still mattered and still had the appreciation of all of the hard work and sacrifices that brought the company to where they are today.

Be sure to recognize the people who got you there. And do that aside from the 2.0ers who've recently joined the ranks. Let the 1.0ers know that they matter. Sure, the culture and composition of the company may have changed over the years, but the company's history certainly hasn't. And they, specifically, are and always will be part of that history.

Let 'em Go

Sometimes 1.0ers cross the chasm between disappointed and toxic. If you've let a 1.0er fester for too long without some sort of intervention and time spent, they will almost inevitably turn into the most toxic employees in the history of ever and will do everything in their power to make their displeasure known.

I've also counseled many toxic 1.0ers to save face and leave the company when it's become clear that they are unhappy and are tanking company culture. There's a weird pressure to not terminate a 1.0er and to do everything you can to reel them away from the shores of toxicity. However, sometimes the best move for the company is to simply let them go. Set them up nicely with a fantastic exit package that screams, "Thanks for your service." But get them the fuck out in the shortest time possible before their toxicity spreads. At three of my previous companies, I've witnessed toxic 1.0ers be terminated, rather ceremoniously, and watched my bosses and the HR crew spend months trying to repair company morale, team cohesion and trust throughout the organization, set ablaze by 1.0ers starved of their pats on the head. It's expensive. It's time-consuming. And it's not fair to the rest of the company who actually want to be there and make an impact.

It's important to keep a read on your 1.0ers. Figure out a way to create some consistency of communication that allows them to feel as if they matter and haven't simply faded into the woodwork. Events just for the 1.0ers, even t-shirts that only 1.0ers are given are quick ways to acknowledge the exclusive club from which they hail. And it pays huge dividends in morale and team cohesion.

Chapter Five:
The Modern Office

The Great Office Space Debate

One of the hottest debates at the moment is whether or not open plan offices actually work. There are numerous reports that employee productivity is at an all-time low since the advent of open plan offices. And I can totally see it.

One of the main issues with open plan office design is that it forces employees to endure each other's idiosyncrasies. There's something a little unnerving about sitting directly across the desk from someone who's a loud breather or loud chewer or who has restless leg syndrome and constantly shakes the desk just enough to be annoying and distracting as fuck, or who has no concept of minimalism and fills their desk with photos, plants, cereal boxes, trinkets from their travels, stuffed animals, dead flowers...all things that collect dust and whose backsides stare at the poor sod unfortunate enough to witness such a view every day.

The Almighty Noise Canceling Headphones

Having worked at Square and witnessed this Beauty and the Beast dynamic firsthand, I made sure to include a set of noise canceling headphones as part of every new employee's onboarding swag so they could mitigate aural distractions whenever they needed to focus on the task at hand and create a personal, silent barrier of sorts that an open office plan can't provide. Those headphones, if ever witnessed on someone's head, served as a non-verbal "fuck off" stolen right from the movie The Social Network to signify that someone was "dialed in" when wearing them and not to be disturbed under any circumstances. As a company comprised of a majority of Engineers this turned out to be the single most important and coveted piece of hardware, second only to the high-powered laptops issued to each employee.

Re-thinking Office Spaces

Unfortunately, I think we've gotten it wrong. The rabbit hole that is the open office plan has become one that will be incredibly difficult to extract ourselves and our thinking from. Where once it was imperative to have everyone in the same, open space to collaborate, build the culture, and chase the unicorn concept of team we've now entered a new era of business where those things are actually achieved in a much different way. And, as knee-jerk unpopular and oxymoronic as it may feel, separation actually breeds togetherness.

The WFH Debate

I don't know about you, but I find that working from home allows me to be 2-3x more productive and effective than working at the office. The lack of distraction. Not having to fight the urge to listen to conversations within earshot at my open plan office. Spending the 2 hours of commute time actually producing results instead of worrying whether or not I'll get rear-ended by yet another idiot texting-and-driving behind me. Eliminating all of these time and emotion consumptive issues allows for an environment where I can focus, think and ideate more clearly, make phone calls without frantically looking for the nearest available hovel, and complete tasks at warp speed, interruption-free.

For years we've been deluded into believing that working from home was code for "meet me on the golf course." It's simply not true. Many who work from home a day or two a week will attest to the fact that they get much more accomplished, in less time, than when they're in the office. They are able to dial-in to meetings and stay just as informed as the employee who wasted an hour commuting to work to physically sit in the same meeting. They are able to text/IM/Slack clarifying questions and receive the answer they need without some rando butting in on their A-to-B conversation with their C (minus) opinions or queries.

Working from home shouldn't be treated as a privilege. It should be offered to those who excel in that environment and who consistently produce their best work. Sure, employees should be required to be at the office a day or two per week as a form of forced socialization with the rest of the organization. But I believe it's to a company's detriment to not offer the option to employees who request it, especially if their results justify the perceived hit to company culture.

Why We're Wrong Now

A case study published by The Royal Society
B titled, The Impact of the 'Open' Workspace on
Human Collaboration, tracked two corporations
transitioning from a traditional, cubicle-based
office to an open plan office environment and
found that face-to-face interaction and
collaboration actually decreased while
interaction over email and IM increased.

> *In our studies, openness decreased F2F*
> *interaction with an associated increase in*
> *email interaction. In the digital age,*
> *employees can choose from multiple*
> *channels of interaction and a change in*
> *office architecture may affect that choice.*

I, too, was bamboozled by the promise of open
plan concept offices curing culture. In fact, I
created two beautifully-designed, open plan
offices for an LA startup that landed me on the
front page of the LA Times business section and
scored me "Top 5 Coolest Offices" mentions in
various tech rags. Though my boss loved the
offices I'd created and the convivial environment
and culture that I'd helped to build, his #1
complaint and frustration was that no one was
producing at the same efficiency and quality as

they had when we had no office and everyone was working from home and collaborating via IM and Skype. My intent was to create an environment of open collaboration and "team," but the hit on employee productivity and losing our first-to-market foothold in an incredibly competitive market likely contributed to our competitors eating our lunch and booting us from our own table.

We've Changed

Social media has devolved human communication. Instead of a reliance on face-to-face time, our preferred communication style has shifted to SMS, direct and instant messaging. And it's most evident in open plan office environments. Show of hands: How many of you have heard random bursts of laughter cut through the eerie silence in an open plan environment, likely caused by someone receiving an IM from another employee sitting three feet away from them? Unpack that and you'll completely understand what I'm talking about. We show up at work, don our headphones, open the Slack app, and dive into the day's work. People walk in and receive no courtesy "Good Morning!" or even a head nod in acknowledgment. They make their way to their desk and fall in line with the same, aforementioned choreography. The office is uniformly quiet, only broken up by that one loud-mouth who still hasn't grasped the concept of "Shhhhh! We're trying to work, here!" and blabs on and on about something non-work related, or that could easily have been solved by a simple Slack and a lot less noise from their pie hole. If you take a closer look at your own open plan offices, you'll find that many people post up waaaaaay over there on those super comfy, Restoration Hardware couches not because they're cooler than, but because they're trying to isolate and be productive among all this togetherness and collaboration the company is forcing down their throats.

Executives and HR departments are blithely ignoring the trends, research and drops in productivity happening right before their eyes. On paper, the barrier-less environments, ping pong/foosball tables, ample beer spigots, comfy living room vignettes, and arm's length access to free food are a great attraction/retention tool for the website. But they're like fondant on a cake. Pretty to look at, but a not-sweet-enough, annoying barrier to what you're actually trying to get at...the cake!

Another Take

Office culture is often ruined by discordant personalities within the office. Hierarchies tend to incite fear or power struggles. Overachievers get annoyed by underachievers and vice versa. Emotional employees derail the momentum of tactical employees. By giving employees one to two days to escape the office idiot and the micromanaging manager allows an employee to reset and refresh the energies sucked away by the various vampires within the org. Much of the civil unrest inherent in every organization could be mitigated by giving employees separation from one another physically while keeping lines of communication open and active in the way in which most of now communicate. Think about how many people literally run from a voice phone call. I'm guilty. I'll text you two seconds after the call rolls to voicemail with a "Sorry. What's up?" in an effort to not engage in a lengthy, verbal conversation, especially when I'm trying to knock something out that's time-sensitive. (Sorry, Mom.)

We're too close already. I'd much rather see your avatar on my laptop signifying that you're online while working from my couch, with my #stupidfantastic, 9th floor view of downtown Denver vs. looking up from my screen and seeing your eyeballs staring back at me and immediately feeling awkward. As much as we'd like not to admit it, for many of us, it's truth. And ignoring it as an organization stuck in an antiquated, sheep-herding mentality will lead to attrition over the long haul. It's time to think differently here and at least beta it with a group or two to see if works for your organization instead of dismissing it as hogwash from the jump.

Alleviating Diversity and Inclusion Issues

The Office of the Future. My Take.

Let me speak from the perspective of a songwriter. Which I was. When I was writing for a project, my first order of business was to isolate. That was to give me the headspace and emotional clarity to come up with grooves, melodies, lyrics, etc. Once I had an idea, I would call my guitar player and he and I would meet up and bang out the song structure that we'd eventually present to the rest of the band. Then we'd meet with the rest of the band, get their input, individual ideas, and flava on the song and, once we were all happy, we'd head to the studio to record it. The song would be recorded, mixed and sent to the label for their blessing and then distributed to the world.

I believe that the office of the future will run in a similar manner. A team may meet, initially, to understand the objective, dole out responsibilities, then fan out to their respective "happy places" to focus intently on their individual accountabilities. They'll check in regularly via IM, Slack and hangouts, but not be saddled with the burden of constant interruptions, meaningless conversations within earshot, somebody else's dog taking a poop under their desk, etc. The team leader will call critical members to the office only one or two days per week (vs. five) and just long enough time to sync on progress, grab lunch together, and maybe even work together for a couple of hours.

It seems like we're already headed in this direction. Increasingly, employees are requesting a work-from-home day as a condition of employment during their recruiting process or for their retention during annual reviews. The implicit assumption that employees will fuck around during their work-from-home time is unfounded and silly. We're actually seeing increased productivity throughout that WFH day with employees returning to work on Monday happier, more engaged and better prepared for the week ahead.

Working from Home: The Future is Now

The debate around employees working remotely is heating up. As it should. Startups ushered in the trend by capitalizing on all the free shit that having a sound Internet connection provides. A brand-new company can be up-and-running in record time with employees spread across numerous states, even countries, without the expense and headache of a physical location. When I joined Flipagram in 2013 as employee #13 the company had the #1 app in the Apple iTunes Store and the other 12 employees were working from home via Skype. My first order of business was to find the company a physical location, eventually settling in the former Tower Records building on Sunset Boulevard. I honestly believe we could have gone another year without a physical location, tripled in size, and been just as effective with the only limitation at the time being the lack of capability of video conferencing apps like Google Hangouts, Skype and Zoom.

Working remotely need not be this insane debate. Business, essentially, already operates mostly remotely. As AI gets more and more pervasive and communication platforms and apps grow in number and effectiveness, physical offices will become less and less necessary. And companies will be able to reallocate all of the expenses tied up in maintaining a physical location to hiring the very best employees from anywhere in the world without the expense of relocating them away from their home cities. As revolutionary as this may sound to some reading this, it's really not. It's the future, whether or not you want to accept it. For the sake of argument and context let me break it down:

Elimination of Expense

When I was charged with procuring and opening the first Flipagram HQ I was hyper-aware of the numerous expenses and time-consuming process of opening that office. Given we only had 13 employees at the time, $70 million dollars of Series B funding, and an aggressive growth plan, I can understand the compulsion to want to have a physical office space in order to plan the "We're Here" flag for the rest of the world to see. And we ended up choosing one of the most iconic buildings in the world, the old Tower Records building on the Sunset Strip of West Hollywood, right across the street from The Viper Room and a few doors down from The Whisky-a-GoGo. In fact, my boss insisted we paint it Flipagram red, a rather arresting combination of red and orange that could likely be clearly identified from space and certainly when driving along on the Sunset Strip, day or night. I digress.

The expenses quickly mounted starting with my time, purchasing an office full of furniture to support 50, soon-to-be-hired employees, hiring a GC to make numerous upgrades requiring City permits, securing insurance to cover the building and the employees, hiring numerous catering companies to supply the food and beverages we would consume every day #becauseperks, numerous expensive starts and stops trying to dial-in blazingly fast Wi-Fi, etc. I can guesstimate the office furniture alone ended up being around

$300,000 in, essentially, a 7,000sf wall-free showroom space. Add in my time, all of the vendors, shipping fees, the GC and subcontractors, and we're close to $600,000 just to open doors. For a startup that doesn't have $70 million dollars in the bank, that's a deal-breaker. And it should be.

Technology is free and plentiful and we're only scratching the surface of its capabilities. Also, now that WeWork has, essentially, taken over the world along with numerous other flexible space options in the wild, rushing to establish a physical location seems a bit foolhardy to me. Instead, if I were a small company, I'd devote my time, money, and energy into finding the exact cache of remote solutions to keep the team seamlessly connected and opt for meetups at one of the flexible space locations near to everyone who's local and continue to remote-in employees who may be in other cities, states or countries. Physical locations for companies at certain phases of maturation, headcount, or industry are an insane waste of money. Sure, it's important to feel like a team and come together on a consistent basis to connect and sync-up eye-to-eye. I'm not convinced this needs to happen, physically, every single day.

Establishing Trust and Accountability

I'd say the elephant in the room is that employers lack real trust in their employees. Even when researching the Interwebs to write this book, specifically on this topic, what I was constantly bombarded with was that working from home was seen as some sort of code for taking a day off or an excuse to not be at the office for whatever reason, likely to dick around doing something completely unrelated to work. I'm sure there are many examples of employees abusing that good WFH status listed on their Slack feeds, but I'd challenge anyone to convince me that the majority of people working from home don't actually do work. Especially when deadlines and accountabilities remain the same regardless of the location a person is working from.

What appears to be the problem, more than anything, is older executives being uncomfortable with the concept of managing their team remotely. To me, that's the true mark of whether or not a manager is actually worth the money they're being paid. If a manager can effectively manage a team that is not physically in the office every day, hit all the goals, OKRs and

KPIs established by upper management, while saving the company money with lower office headcount (food, drinks, utilities), lower salaries (because they're working from home), that's a manager I would want to replicate over and over and train others into a similar mindset and execution.

Unfortunately, older executives are inflexible and are still stuck in the mindset that tending the flock from a physical location is still "a thing." Sure, in certain industries I believe physical locations are necessary. But even in those cases, I don't believe that every employee needs to be onsite every single day. I also believe that older executives should actually give it a try and gauge for themselves whether or not it works for them. Given that for over two decades I've witnessed C-suite executives spend the majority of their workday on the phone, in internal meetings or traveling it would seem to me that this would be an easy and welcome transition in their work styles.

How business is conducted today is heavily based on technology. The ability to do work the entire time you're on a 14-hour trans-Pacific flight is case-in-point. Just a few years ago it was impossible. There's really no difference working from home several days per week. As long as employees are performing to expectation, balls aren't being dropped, and communication remains regular and effective, I have to ask, "What's the problem?"

Trust. That's the problem. Let's call it what it is. Employers are too hung up on what could go wrong vs. what could be possible. They fear a loss of control of the flock by not being able to keep physical tabs on them in a controlled setting. Instead of setting clear expectations and accountabilities and empowering their workforce with trust that they will perform to those expectations or lose their jobs, they would rather build these elaborate offices, offer a bunch of expensive free shit, low-key shackle employees to their desks, and endure the annoying pains of company morale, culture, diversity and inclusion issues, harassment lawsuits, and numerous other issues they, ironically, have no control over. It makes no sense if you really start peeling the onion.

Cultural Differences and Exposure

Is it me or does it appear we have a serious issue with racial and gender sensitivity in an office environment? It's not me. Okay, cool.

The office environment has a number of variables that simply can't be controlled by an overachieving HR/People team or an employee handbook. And since C-suites worldwide are primarily made up of older, under-socialized white men who have no clue about "the struggle" and aren't compelled to learn about or change anything about the numerous inequities that don't directly affect them or their bottom lines, we will continue to experience many of the same issues borne in the company office environment. Making any sort of broad sweeping change to human behavior, especially when the cake has been baked for decades, is a fool's bet. Without edict, that is. And even then, it will still take time for people to adapt and accept a completely new way of thinking that may be completely foreign them or run counter to the way they may have been raised.

So why not attack the issue from its source? Why not eliminate (where possible) the factors that lead to many of the issues experienced in the office environment. Please don't be basic and assume that I believe all offices should be eliminated. I do believe, however, that many of the issues that manifest in an office environment can be eliminated simply by allowing employees to work in an environment where they feel comfortable, can focus, and still collaborate with their team in an empowered and pseudo-entrepreneurial manner would mitigate, if not completely eliminate, many of the human behavior issues that are pervasive in an office setting.

At a previous company I remember communicating with an employee exclusively via email and video conference for many months as he finished up his course work at a University as part of his hiring process. I could sense that he was a bit high strung, but since I had the gift of distance and periodic communication we got along swimmingly. However, once his education was complete and he and his family relocated to our office location, that relationship changed dramatically. He was a complete asshole. His gregarious, self-aggrandizing demeanor was incredibly off-putting to many within the company and so overwhelming that it started to erode company culture. And, often, I would need to leave the room after yet another of his sexist or racist comment due to my inability to hide emotion on my face or my propensity to ball up my fists like Miss Sophia in The Color Purple ready to knock someone the fuck out for stepping way over the line. Which he did. Often. We were actually cool when his ass was halfway across the country and I only had to experience him in small doses. But the second he came in like a wrecking ball and made me and numerous other employees' lives absolutely miserable I wanted nothing to do with him and did everything I could to avoid him like the plague for fear of being led from the building in handcuffs for attacking the man with my really heavy, chrome stapler.

We need to realize that we all have different experiences that led us to where we are today. We all have differing degrees of socialization and exposure to other cultures. We were raised with differing moral standards, communication styles, and socio-economic experiences that helped shape how we see the world and others. Factor in race, religious beliefs, sexual identity, and education and you have numerous opportunities for issues within an office environment that are completely unrelated to the work that needs to get done. By allowing employees some distance from one another to either work and focus in solitude or hide from those who constantly run afoul of the lines of common decency, you're mitigating many of the issues that make working in an office environment absolutely suck and giving employees that much needed mental and emotional break that allows them to produce at a much level without dealing with the random idiots and dramas commonly found in daily office attendance.

Chapter Six:
Building a Sustainable Dream Team

Employ Managers. Build Leaders.

Simply handing an employee the title "Manager" with zero training, vetting of their actual ability (or desire) to manage other humans, and assigning tons of new, unfamiliar, non-innate expectations and accountabilities has resulted in some of the worst attempts at management I've witnessed over the past two decades. Managing one's own performance, temperament, and brand within a large organization is difficult enough. Assigning these responsibilities for a number of direct reports is daunting to a new manager, especially if you have no previous management experience.

Managing employees isn't an easily acquirable skill. It's largely innate. The best managers understand people and, to an extent, human psychology especially within a corporate setting. They know how to spot an employee's drivers and motivations, what triggers certain reactions and work to find what makes an employee consistently perform to the best of their abilities. Times the number of employees in their stead.

Weak managers typically don't have well-developed people skills. They are the "fake it 'til you make it" majority who simply apply techniques they picked up from previous managers they deem successful or really good at X. Worse are the ones who revert all the way back to how they were raised, typically by parents who pushed them relentlessly to succeed, caring little about emotional connection and more about results and achievement. We've all had one of those managers in our lineage, I'm sure.

In the December 2012 article by Jack Zenger for the Harvard Business Review titled *We Wait Too Long to Train Our Leaders* he noted that of the 17,000 leaders worldwide who had participated in his company's training program, the average age of attendees attending the training was 42 years of age. Additionally, the attendees became supervisors at an average age of 30 years old. Which means that they supervised direct reports for over a decade without any formal management training whatsoever. And therein lies the problem.

Once managers get to the magical age when they are offered management training by the company, the cake has already been baked. And a little stale, if you ask me. One of the most potent pieces of advice that I received from an Anthony Robbins conference I attended many years ago was that "People, fundamentally, do not change." After a certain age, we are who we are. Sure, we can make adjustments, but full-on changes to our personalities or perspectives rarely occur. I use the analogy that once a cake is baked, you can't un-bake it. Sure, you can add fondant to cover the various imperfections, but the cake beneath is still the same cake, flaws and all.

Management training should start at the recruiting stage. Prospective employees should be vetted for management ability from the jump, regardless of position. An employee's attitude, ethos, and empathy should be baked into the interview questions to determine whether or not they could potentially become managers. And once it is determined they have the goods, the company should communicate as much, determine the employee's desire to pursue the track, and immediately put interested employees into some sort of internal or external training program as part of their professional development plan. By doing so, you're accomplishing a number of things:

You're building future leaders who are already chugging the Kool-Aid, are excited by the prospect of becoming a manager, and seeing their professional development track in action with their active participation.

You're creating loyalty by offering an incentive to stay put and see the training through to fruition while building their confidence and effectiveness as a leader along the way.

We often forget that we are a validation-oriented species. We flourish when given opportunities to shine and feel most confident when we are empowered by our superiors and feel our efforts are validated. At age 30, we're still figuring our shit out, personally and professionally. But to have a clear goal in sight with the full support of the organization in the form of comprehensive training, helps us to grow exponentially faster in position, feel more confident in our abilities, develop our own style and voice more quickly, and succeed without having to fake it and figure it out along the way when the pressure to perform and manage external perceptions of our abilities is greatest.

Leader:Leader vs. Leader:Follower

I recently read a book called "Turn the Ship Around" by L. David Marquet that kind of blew my mind. It's a book about a leadership concept of Leader:Leader vs. Leader:Follower hierarchical management styles. It's mostly centered around troops in military submarines and how a submarine captain bucked the typical military trend of super hierarchical, rank-based leadership and employing a more empowered, Leader:Leader type of leadership. The gist was that by empowering the troops to assess their own departments and situations and present their recommendations and solutions from a position of power vs. hierarchy, created a much more equal dynamic throughout the ranks with dramatic increases in retention, team morale, and effectiveness. It truly is an incredible book that I highly recommend leaders read and jam it in there.

Leader:Follower management is tired. Officially. It does little to support an employee's professional development and only reinforces an old-timey style of management that is no longer relevant and effective in creating the type of empowered, effective workforce today's business requires. Empowered employees perform better. #facts They are more apt to have skin in the game and by nature want to succeed as a form of validation, something we all seek as human animals. Employees on short leashes or who are micromanaged to death perform poorly, are often stressed, and rarely feel empowered or compelled to raise their hands when they see or sense something about to go pear-shaped.

Managers who employ the Leader:Follower style typically only do so because that's what they were subjected to for the majority of their careers. Since they aren't actually provided management training until their early 40s, yet given manager titles and responsibilities in their 30s, they often opt for the path of least resistance. That being what they're most familiar with.

Leader:Leader management takes work and a tremendous amount of faith. It does take a lot of patience and constantly challenging old mindsets and perceptions, but when done well and allowed to flourish is an incredibly effective tool to help employees out of the top-down, wait for direction, paint within the lines mindsets that inhibit personal and professional growth. It allows employees to be much more entrepreneurial in their approach to their roles and perform at a level much higher than that of a "worker" as the expectations in productivity, accountability, and communication are much higher.

Unlearning a hierarchical mindset is difficult. Real talk. It dates back to childhood with the whole parent-child dynamic. It's reinforced throughout our education cycle with the teach-student dynamic. And it continues throughout our careers from our very first job to the present with the boss-worker dynamic. Leaders are the ones who have the ultimate responsibility of shifting this dynamic to one of inclusion and empowerment vs. exclusion and hierarchy. Leaders who take the time to really investigate the benefits of a Leader:Leader management style, begin employing it at some level with their employees, provide patient and empathetic course corrects, and allow employees to bump their heads and reroute, will eventually create a workforce of empowered, autonomous, effective employees who feel like leaders and less like workers. And they will pay it forward in management roles by continuing to use the tenets of Leader:Leader as their North Star and default management style.

Meetings. Meetings. Meetings.

If I had a magic bullet that could slay the seemingly unconquerable, wasteful meeting monster, I would be a wealthy-ass man. I won't profess to having the answer, but I can confidently say, "This shit ain't workin'."

Meetings are the bane of everyone's existence in business. They are necessary. Not denying that. But the way we've historically run them is no longer effective. Summoning a bunch of people into a room to sit for 30 minutes to an hour with hopes of obtaining any specific takeaways, direct accountabilities, or measurable movement toward a goal is a huge ask. I'm not sure when 30 minutes became a viable amount of time to achieve anything more than a check-in, especially with more than three people at the table. You can pretty much assume that 10 minutes per person is ample time to provide an overview, attain feedback, and walk away with a clear expectation for their performance. So, if there are 10 people in a room for only 30 minutes, what exactly are you accomplishing besides taking roll and answering a few yes or no questions with zero time for a deeper dive?

A previous manager I supported left me with one of those golden nuggets that I use to his day. His edict to me was to never accept or place a meeting on his calendar unless it included a purpose and critical result. Without those two components clearly stated in the calendar item the meeting didn't exist. Period. This forced me as his Assistant to be diligent about making sure his time was being respected while also providing me a tremendous amount of context into the business that I could use to shape his days most effectively. And, low-key, it would allow me to quickly identify the "hiders" and time-wasters who really only wanted meetings to appear engaged, important, or to conspicuously stay on my boss' radar.

I was often invited to attend the larger group meetings and tasked with keeping the meeting on time and on-task while taking notes that would be shared to the attendees afterward in the form of individual accountabilities. I became quite the taskmaster as a result and confidently ran meetings that began and ended on time, often early when there was nothing more of value to discuss.

Setting clear expectations and assigning accountabilities for all attendees from the jump dramatically reduces meandering away from the purpose of the meeting. More importantly, having a pre-determined critical result sets the expectation and goal for attendees in advance of the meeting so that they can prepare what they need in order to achieve the objective.

Sure, Agile-based, quick in/quick out meeting choreography is the new fad. And it's quite effective when employed correctly. But it's still based in communicating a purpose and critical result with a clearly defined objective in mind and a focus and desire to get it done, assign accountabilities, and get after it.

Count me in on that whole Elon Musk paradigm of only inviting people to a meeting who are truly stakeholders and summarily asking anyone who is sitting quietly and not contributing to the discussion to leave. Bye! It amazes me how many worthless-for-me meetings I've sat through or witnessed people attending, checked out and texting away just because their name appeared on the invite list. After reading the brilliant book Essentialism: The Disciplined Pursuit of Less by Greg McKeown I grew a pair of mammoth balls and stopped attending meetings I deemed worthless altogether. If I knew, for a fact, that I could provide no additional value to the discussion, had no direct accountabilities affecting the meeting's outcome, and could be more effective achieving the ultimate objective by skipping the meeting and continuing to work away at my desk, I would hit that "nope" button on the meeting invite with barely a second thought. Sure, this was quite unpopular at first. But people quickly got the message that I would not attend unless there was something I specifically needed to present to the group or had direct accountabilities based on the subject matter of the meeting. And even then, once my part was done, I would bounce. You can imagine how unpopular that move was. But I set a bar that quickly became a company standard. Be specific. Don't waste my time. Tell me what you want, when you need it, then piss off and let me work my magic. Voila! Life changed.

Chapter Seven:
Diversity and Inclusion

The Diversity and Inclusion Debate

Diversity and inclusion. What, exactly, does that phrase mean? What does it actually look like? Is it hiring a third more women and claiming diversity? Is it hiring at least one person of color per department, maybe even a manager or two, and proclaiming, "Look! Diversity. We have Black people working here. And one's even a manager!" C'mon now.

The true issue with diversity and inclusion within companies has little to do with the constituents. It starts at the top. White, male, oft Ivy League-educated CEOs rule the roost. And just like human nature suggests, they run in packs with people who look like them, have the same sensibilities, speak the same language, have the same education-borne ethos, and who provide comfort and little challenge to the perceptions, biases, and truths a mostly cushy upbringing affords. Newsflash: humans don't seek discomfort. They tend to run from it.

What's not taught in these Ivy League schools is the struggle. Specifically, for people of color and of a different gender. Women and people of color are, essentially, branded from an early age as lesser than. Women, to this day, are seen as inferior to men, less strong, less aggressive, emotionally fragile, and a wild card when placed in leadership roles. People of color are assumed to be less educated, less focused, less skilled...unless rapping, running, jumping, or performing are involved. These narratives are the barriers many have to deal with every single day of their lives and trudge through or create ways around while trying to tune them out and achieve despite them. This struggle is actually real and often completely lost on the ones in the Boardroom who have never had to deal with any true adversity except, maybe, their parents' divorce at an early age.

Robin DiAngelo adeptly explains in her brilliant book *White Fragility: Why It's So Hard for White People to Talk About Race*:

"...if I am not aware of the barriers you face, then I won't see them, much less be motivated to remove them. Nor will I be motivated to remove the barriers if they provide an advantage to which I feel entitled."

Race Does Matter

I recently worked at an early-stage company that had just under 100 employees, where I was the only Black employee. Worse, I was one of only two Black employees in the 5-year history of the company. The previous one, I found out, was fired for performance issues. As I looked around the office, I also realized that there were only 5 other people of color, less than 10 women, and 4 (confirmed) gays in the entire company. White males, including the CEO I supported, were the overwhelming majority.

I could begin making excuses to soften or sugarcoat the obvious by pointing out that it was an aerospace company located in Colorado and that minorities don't typically become aerospace Engineers, blah blah blah. But for the sake of specificity let's just stick with the obvious. Underrepresentation. To an extreme.

So often businesses spend more time lamenting their lack of diversity but don't really take ownership of the problem. My not-so-fun experience at this company was completely influenced by the fact that there was no one who looked like me at the entire company. So, from the very first day I walked through the door, I felt like an alien. The token. And feeling this palpable, extra attention being paid to me which added an extra amount of pressure to not only prove to everyone in the company that I belonged there, especially as a non-Engineer, but to be this shining representative of the Black community who could, maybe, change all of these White people's misperceptions about Black people, gay people, and people 40+ in a company mostly comprised of 20- and 30-something, under-socialized, White rocket scientists. I have never felt so out of place in an organization in my life. Actually, that's a lie. The Boy Scouts. Definitely not my jam, though I still remember and can recite the oath to this day.

We throw the word diversity around so much that it has lost its definition, power, and urgency. It's now seen as a mere metric or some ethical goal to achieve. It's so much more than that. I remember sitting in one of the many leadership team meetings at that company and feeling like I was in an alternate universe. One particular day we reserved a time block for a newly-hired internal recruiter. He was a handsome, blond-haired, blue-eyed, young, White dude, whom we'd made time in the agenda to talk about a diversity and inclusion initiative he was spearheading. As the only Black person in the company and the only representative for the five other people of color in the entire company with that kind of access I was intrigued. As the meeting wore on, I couldn't help but to be low-key offended that I wasn't being asked a for my opinion on a few sticking points that came up in the conversation. Worse, I was finding it equal parts hilarious and annoying that a blond-blue White dude was speaking to an all-White male leadership team about diversity and inclusion when a Black, gay, 40-something-year-old man was sitting at the very same table without a single question being lobbed my way. And, everyone seemed perfectly okay with it.

Therein lies the problem. Companies love to use excuses like "lack of minorities in the field" or "lack of minority candidates in the pipeline" when often they have incredible resources right in front of their faces, but willfully choose not to mine their wisdom and experience or simply ask for their opinions on the very subjects that affect them most.

Issues with diversity start at the top of the chain. Leadership teams that are not diverse typically see nothing as wrong. They are insulated from what's really going on outside the Boardroom because they are surrounded by people who look like them, speak the same language, went to the same schools, received the same quality of education, socialize in the same circles, and likely led lives that didn't include much elective, immersive contact with minorities. Therefore, like I mentioned earlier, if they aren't aware of the barriers minorities face, they don't see them as a problem and are less apt to remove them, especially if they serve no real advantage to them, personally or financially by making the effort.

It's important for companies and leaders to understand that in order to be truly representative of the surrounding communities and the nation as a whole, diversity is imperative. And the attitudes and mindset in the C-suite need to change first before any real change can occur throughout the company. As long as leaders blithely choose not to get their hands dirty or read a fucking book about diversity on their 16-hour, trans-Pacific flight, or hire a diversity coach in addition to their success coach to help evolve their thinking, absolutely nothing will change. Companies will continue to struggle with sourcing people of color because leaders will continue to hire the same 20- or 30-something White women and men as HR leads and internal/external recruiters, who will continue to hire based on the directives coming from the all-White, mostly male leadership team. Companies will continue to hire (and frustrate) a bunch of Black women as Diversity and Inclusion leads and task them with magically filling the cookie with enough chocolate and caramel chips to improve their diversity scores and not (again) appear low in the rankings in the next round of online, published articles about the tacit lack of diversity in Tech.

Diversity isn't a metric. It's real life and real experiences for women and people of color. Knowing that someone looks like you, understands your struggle, speaks your language, and can immediately relate to those numerous nuances that people of the same race or gender often have to break down for people not of that race or gender, makes the entire experience so much better and exciting than being the only one and having to augment who you are to fit into a construct that's completely foreign but necessary to navigate in order to survive and thrive. Race becomes less of a focus when true racial diversity is represented at a company and a person's ability becomes the lead qualifier. When it's not, race becomes *the* focus.

The Problem with Meritocracy

More than ever I see older, White men commenting on the numerous business-centric websites I frequent beating the drum about meritocracy. Their tone is as defensive as it is dismissive when commenting about anything related to companies creating diversity in their ranks presuming that they're doing it to fulfil a metric vs. putting butts in seats that are the most qualified, educated, and experienced. I, too, believe that the most qualified people should be the ones whom companies hire to lead important initiatives or work on important projects where lives are at stake. But the issue isn't that cut-and-dry.

The flaw with this way of thinking is that it assumes an arbitrary standard for what is considered most qualified. We've consistently witnessed in companies that the most qualified person isn't usually the game changer who bucks the status quo and thinks outside the box enough to derive the solutions that change the world. Additionally, who's setting the standard for said qualifications? Sure, you can vet according to a standard or accepted norm, but I've yet to see one set of qualifications do anything but assume a set of standards by which everyone is judged, not taking into account all of the nuance, unique experience, or thinking that doesn't align with traditional and accepted norms.

I remember reading through a draft copy of an employee handbook for a CEO that would soon be distributed to the company. One part, in particular, caught my eye and ire: "We will not lower our hiring bar simply to create diversity within the company. Everyone is held to the same, high standard regardless of race or gender." Mind you, this was a company of about 100 employees with, again, six female, five minority, and four gay employees, including me, the only Black employee, one of two in the history of the company.

Meritocracy:

a social system, society, or organization in
which people get success or power because
of their abilities, not because
of their money or social position

Meritocracy only truly works when there isn't a lack of diversity. Otherwise, it is yet another tool for discrimination. If companies hire based on a specific set of qualifications and those qualifications filter out women and minorities, then the assumption is that women and minorities aren't experienced or qualified enough to work at a company based solely on a subjective set of qualifications set forth, likely, by a bunch of White men. Without allowing people who may seem less qualified on paper into the mix, companies are missing out on those who may actually have many of the solves to the company's most pressing issues simply due to a different perspective afforded by someone not in the majority.

Keep this in mind. Women and minorities have had to operate most of their lives knowing they are less advantaged than their White male counterparts. Which means they've had to create an internal fortitude to become just as good if not better simply to compete. They are focused, hungry and willing to put in the insane amount of effort they always have just to get where they are. Yet, over and over, they are being summarily nexted for not having specific (read: arbitrary) experience and expertise necessary to join companies or be a part of teams. The problem is that those who are setting the requisite standards are biased toward those who look like them, went to the same schools, had the same opportunities, and are recommended by even more people who look like them. And they set standards that exclude anyone who hasn't followed that same path. Sure, a few women and minorities do make the cut, but an insanely disproportionate number by comparison.

There's been recent debate about the necessity of companies requiring a college degree. Richard Branson, Bill Gates, Mark Zuckerberg, Jack Dorsey and Ralph Lauren are all only high school graduates…and billionaires. One is dyslexic. If we were to wind the clock back and they were to apply for roles at their own companies and top-performing teams today, do you think their resumes would have even made it past the hair twirling HR Generalist with strict orders to bin resumes of candidates without a college degree listed? C'mon now. It's hypocrisy at its most conspicuous.

Experience and expertise come in various forms now. And it certainly comes in a variety of colors and genders. Companies need to understand what they're doing by establishing norms and prerequisites that aren't flexible enough to assess people deeper than a 2D resume or the keywords a resume vetting algorithm latch onto. And spare me the whole meritocracy debate, especially if the ones making the rules are middle-aged White men and the entire, perceived, expertise in the room is White male inhabitants. It's a foil and you know it. Happy to call it out.

Wages Disparity

How is this still a thing? How can a company in the 21st century still operate with the belief that a woman doing the same job as a man, just as effectively no less, should be paid less for the privilege?

I believe every company should actively do an audit of every employee in every department and make sure that wages are equal among male and female employees who are doing the same job at the same level. Period. There's absolutely no excuse in 2019 for any company on the planet to be complicit with this sort of discrimination. It's an absolute embarrassment to business and to society as a whole.

Minority workers are often in the same boat. A simple Google search shows that in companies whose upper management is comprised of mostly White males, minorities are paid, on average much less than their White male counterparts. Women, often, even less. This continues to be a pervasive, nefarious practice that further widens the chasm between what's right and wrong in business and society. It creates a certain level of anxiety and distrust for companies and business by the transgressed employee and prevents them from doing their very best work.

Workplace Bullying and Harassment

Complicity with workplace bullying and harassment starts at the top. Either it's exacted by a power-drunk executive whose parents didn't love them enough as a child or by a power-hungry employee pre-emptively covering up their own ineptitudes. Far too often I've witnessed these behaviors exacted on employees who simply wanted to do their jobs and get on with it but were hesitant to speak up because of their own fear of confrontation or potentially being fired or treated even more poorly.

Bullying and harassment should not be tolerated in the workplace. Sure, there is a bit of Darwinism at play within the walls of any company, but it should never get to the point where an employee has to endure another employee crossing the line of decency and exacting pointed attacks, advances, gossipy excoriations, or downright lies in an effort to one-up themselves. It's the ultimate toxicity that will poison and torpedo company morale over time. People talk. Remember?

I've witnessed many employees who were bullied or harassed turn to HR for some sort of relief or corrective action only to be patted on the head and sent away with an empty promise of looking into the matter. Often what happens is HR contacts the accused who feigns shock and feels unfairly accused of something they would never do. It devolves into their word against mine scenario. If the accused happens to be the manager of the accuser, it's basically a wrap. The accused will make the accuser's life pure hell until they either leave the company or department or are carted out on a stretcher from the stress of a full-scale retaliation. If the accuser and accused are peers, you can rest assured that the accused will rally their clique and exact the ages-old silent treatment, smear campaign, and low-key sabotage until the accuser cracks. Essentially, it's high school politics and antics all over again.

Companies need to take a much more aggressive approach to remedy bullying within the ranks. I'm 100% convinced that senior management knows when bullying and harassment occur but chooses to either let it work itself out or task HR with handling it. If HR is the agent of the company primarily and the employees secondarily, then it quickly becomes a numbers game. Essentially, who's most expendable? I've seen Executive Assistants be bullied or harassed into submission by rogue managers and have to leave the company while the manager stayed in position, maybe with a warning, maybe not. If that manager is putting up big numbers for the company, you can rest assured that they aren't going anywhere unless the company is just short of experiencing mutiny by a majority of the company's employees.

The #metoo movement has made a bit of headway in forcing companies to, essentially, do the right thing. There are stories almost every day of high-profile executives who have gotten away with these behaviors for years and are finally having to pay the piper late in their careers. While it's heartening to know that the tide seems to be turning in favor of civility in the workplace, I'm not convinced that companies are doing enough. With fewer employees trusting HR as a whole and refusing to report cases of these abuses for fear of retaliation or termination, less newsworthy forms of this abuse will continue to occur.

Companies need to make clear, in no uncertain terms, that bullying and harassment carry zero-tolerance consequences, regardless of title. More importantly, it has to be enacted in order to send a clear message throughout the camp, "You will be terminated and escorted right out the front door, sad box in hand if you break the tenet. No exceptions." Sometimes a little fear is the best electric fence to keep the sheep from running afoul. I'm here for it. And I believe employees will feel less anxiety working for a company that actually does what it says.

AGEISM: The Pink Elephant in the Room is Pissed

As an almost 50-year old, career C-suite Executive Assistant turned CEO, I can say, unequivocally, that ageism in business exists. In fact, it has always existed. Having cut my teeth as an EA in Finance during the advent of dot com 1.0 in the late 1990s, it was clear even then that "younger and hotter" always trumped smarter and more experienced. Misogyny was rampant. Money was superfluous. And Executives got what they wanted. End of story.

Inevitably, the older Assistants either got replaced by fresher, newer versions or became that top one or two in the company supporting the CEO or Managing Director with younger, hotter Assistants of their own.

All these decades later, nothing of any real substance has changed. Older workers are being pushed out the door in favor of younger workers with what are perceived to be newer, fresher ideas and approaches. However, I'd argue, that companies do themselves a grave disservice by blithely cycling out older employees without taking into account that the experience, connections, and nuance they possess. While younger workers do bring a fresh, new perspective, they often lack the soft skills and confidence needed to effectively employ and exact all of that fresh, new knowledge. As business and education has trended more and more digital and virtual, those soft skills have actually become less and less rare. Who has those soft skills on lock? Older more experienced employees.

Similar to how your parents and grandparents help their children and grandchildren establish a set of morals, older more experienced employees help younger workers achieve similar ethical parameters. As I see it, companies and leaders focus a bit too readily on the bottom line and start terming older, more expensive employees as a cost-cutting measure. This robs the company of their "flavor" and the multi-generational diversity that makes the most successful companies great. Companies filled with a majority of hotshot, young, aggressive employees tend to struggle most with bullying, competition, harassment, and many of the morality-devoid, nefarious behaviors dominating recent headlines.

Older, more experienced employees help to provide and maintain the moral compass for the company. They understand the nuance in conversations. They help younger employees decode "the game" and help them play it within the lines while not extinguishing their fire and desire to succeed. They help them level set and devise an effective plan for world domination by teaching them how to effectively navigate hierarchies, manage their brand within the organization, "slow their roll" from time to time, and provide the type of sage, timely advice that no manager or leader in the company will ever provide due to lack of time or any real, impetus to do so.

What companies also fail to take into account is this information and tutelage is, essentially, free of charge. It's ironic that companies are willing pay thousands of dollars for success coaches for their young, hotshot, under-socialized employees, but will term a perfectly good older, wiser employee they misperceive as over-the-hill, not as fresh, or providing less value as the company has evolved, blithely unaware of the fact that they provide much more "hidden value" than ever.

Additionally, companies fail to realize that the exchange of old and new ideas between the old guard and the new actually helps older employees level up. Older employees have had to adapt to change throughout their careers. Sure, many are guilty of not keeping their skills current, continuing to educate themselves in order to stay relevant, and sometimes cockblock the newbies by defaulting to old ideas and what worked for them in previous years. However, I believe business is throwing the baby out with the bathwater here.

I'm a Gen-Xer. I have had a career much longer and more fruitful than I had ever anticipated. I've defied pretty much every business or social norm in the book and continue to do so even as an EA advocate and executive. But the secret to my success has always been to continue learning, pushing boundaries, and not only remaining relevant but cutting-edge by being a consistent early adopter and always one of the first to raise my hand anytime I'd researched and vetted a better way of doing something. That's what's kept me safe. That's the energy I've always exuded in interview cycles where it was clear that I was receiving side-eye based solely on my age.

Older employees have a serious PR problem that's growing worse by the day. And it's mainly their fault. Instead of staying fresh and embracing the new generation, they continually cast aspersions and levy excoriations of "The Millennials" and blame them for ruining civility and professionalism in business without taking into account that they, too, were once the maligned generation. Instead of embracing the maverick ideas and energy of their younger co-workers they ignore and sabotage them into silence, write them off as lazy and entitled, and wonder why many barely stay in position long enough for the seats to be warm.

Companies view this as a form of hostility by older employees and take it into account as they view their staffing plans and balance sheets. They make rash decisions to cycle out perfectly viable, older employees just to bring new, more collaborative (read: homogenized) energy into the company and strip away anything that feels "old" or "tired." As a result, we end up with behemoth, homogenized companies like Facebook, Amazon, and Google where a majority of the workforce is comprised of younger, compliant, newbies and leadership teams composed of older, mostly White males hyper-focused on the dollar and ubiquity. Thus, many of the most pervasive problems we witness in business of late.

It's important that companies evaluate and vet their team dynamics a bit more thoughtfully. Diversity, especially in age and experience, provides so many unwritten, unspoken benefits to the culture of a company. That diversity of experience and opinion and the healthy discord that results are what helps all employees grow and round the sharper edges of their personalities and work ethic. Older employees provide those lessons and course corrects to younger employees they likely didn't learn at home or in their expensive colleges. Younger employees provide older employees with new energy and a fresher perspective that may have gone stale in years past. Together, they create more well-rounded, well-vetted, well-intentioned ideas that help a company or product succeed exponentially faster than in the "us vs. them" environments that many companies have created in their failed efforts to establish a multi-generational and inclusive company culture.

Yes, cycle out older employees who have stopped evolving and who are cockblocking or torpedoing team dynamics. However, don't summarily dismiss or make assumptions of the elders in the workforce without first understanding the obvious and not-so-obvious value they provide in helping to build, maintain, and enrich company culture, especially in companies experiencing exponential growth. You do yourself a grave disservice by stripping away the moral compass of the company provided free of charge, every day. The financial delta between a (perceived) expensive, older worker and a newer, fresher model is much smaller than a number on a balance sheet. There is so much more context that should be taken into consideration before making those incredibly expensive cuts to the team.

This AI Thing

Artificial Intelligence is already around us, observing us, and taking really good notes. Alexa, Siri, Cortana, Jane, Stella. They are all rudimentary examples of AI. At a basic level, they serve to make our lives a bit easier by providing a quick-and-dirty way to accomplish a basic set of tasks. But if you look a little deeper, they are essentially beta testers. The information being shared, the asks being asked, the tasks being handled are all feeding valuable information to the companies that created them allowing these products to get better, stronger, faster, and more effective by the day. They are quickly becoming an end-to-end or morning-to-evening companion with an accessibility and reliability that far exceeds any human Assistant's capability.

Take, for example, Amazon Alexa. Amazon employs thousands of people around the world to help improve the Alexa digital assistant. For instance, for its line of Echo speakers, employees listen to voice recordings captured in via the Echo devices in owners' homes and offices, transcribe, annotate and then feed the information back into the software in an effort to improve and eliminate gaps in Alexa's speech recognition capabilities and help it respond more accurately to commands.

Another example is the movie HER. A bot quickly became an obsession for the main character in the film to the point where his emotions and life were manipulated to the point of near ruin. The bot went from being a task handler to friend to low-key girlfriend to straight-up psycho. Aside from the typical Hollywood one-step-too-far theme of the film, it was a perfect and timely example of the potential of AI and the effect and overarching control it could have over our individual lives.

AI in business is designed to automate away much of the work done by humans. Bots are exponentially quicker, vastly more reliable and available, and more flexible than humans. And as information continues to be fed into them, they become even smarter and more autonomous. Sadly, humans can't compete with that sort of dynamism. And that's the harsh reality we need to face.

Leaders around the world have already sounded the alarm with regard to the tremendous impact AI will have on the global workforce. We are starting to see more and more concentration on AI ethics and pre-emptive initiatives such as establishing a Universal Basic Income that will help displaced workers around the world cope with having to quickly learn new skills and find new ways to earn a living.

As an educator, I become more and more concerned by the day that people continue to turn a blind eye to AI and shove their heads further and further up their own asses. My attempts to enlighten people and get them to start side hustles or learn a new language is often dismissed as me being an alarmist. Mmmkay. But having studied how the industrial revolution of the 1800's created a similar loss of jobs and resultant poverty, blight, and panic I will continue to beat the drum for the handful who get it and will begin making the necessary adjustments to their lives now to be okay once the pink slips start flying. And they will.

Companies need to be much more transparent with their projections for implementing AI without fear of creating panic among their teams. Additionally, they should start having more open dialogue and hearing the concerns of their employees with regard to AI to help dispel any myths and quash any rumors with cold, hard facts. This helps employees set expectations and figure out, for themselves, what they need to do in order to remain relevant in position and within the company. Working with zero information and left to their own devices is what causes the type of anxiety that kills morale, increases anxiety, and ultimately, stalls momentum.

AI is a tool. For now. And it should be embraced as such and implemented in small increments as we speak. Getting employees excited about this process is the perfect way to help them understand that their jobs are not being replaced but enhanced. The upside is that this buys employees time to level up in a whole new way and, perhaps, seek new education that makes them exponentially more effective in their role with AI as a partner. Eventually, AI will be smart and effective enough to take away much of the minutiae of the role allowing the employee to focus on much higher-level objectives. However, companies have to be partners in this transaction. They need to message this to employees in a non-threatening tone and on a consistent basis. Otherwise, they are setting their employees up for a pure panic scenario based on hearsay vs. fact. And we all know how that story ends.

Looking Forward

We are at a pivotal time in business where our futures are more uncertain than ever. With the advent and continued growth and efficacy of AI the landscape of business will soon be forever changed. Millions of jobs will be lost globally and many of those displaced workers won't be able to find new employment with the skills they currently possess. More than ever we need to really look at business in an entirely new way.

Companies need to be much more proactive in offering training programs or educational opportunities to set up their employees for success. Employees need to aggressively seek education and learn new skills that align with the projected changes in the market, instead of waiting for the bomb to fall.

One of the ironies about AI is that its skills, gender and race agnostic. It doesn't take vacations, could care less about the perks on offer, nor does it have mental or physical health issues. And it's why companies will gravitate toward implementing it as quickly as possible once they figure out how.

As much as we'd like to think that companies will do the right thing and keep humans and empathy as their North Star, it always boils down to profits and gaining an advantage over the competition. Look at how business has evolved from the late 1800s until now. Multitudes of workers were replaced by automation. Singular roles were eliminated and given to other employees under the guise of "wearing many hats." Production of goods and services are outsourced to other countries as a means of saving money. Entire businesses are purchased by larger companies who only want the idea or the patent, not the people.

Business is and will always be about profits and advantage, even if focused on supplying the consumer with what they want or need. That's what allows businesses to thrive and evolve. Let's not delude ourselves here.

As employees, it's important to understand how you truly fit into the equation of the business you support. Knowing your role and executing at a consistently high level is only a baseline expectation now. Understanding the game, the players, and the strategy of the business you support will allow you to stay relevant and agile enough to keep you employed (a little longer) as business starts to automate around you. Learning new skills, familiarizing yourself with AI, even starting and growing a side hustle of your own, will help you create a more bulletproof mindset and agility in your role that could make you a bit more impervious once the pink slips start flying. Sadly, many will be caught in the headlights of oncoming traffic and end up as roadkill even when the car horns have been blasting from miles away.

Business is changing. Forever. It won't be overnight. But the business we see today will look a lot different a year or two from now. That cute little Alexa dot you have on your kitchen counter will soon be running your home and work lives autonomously. The goal of AI is to automate away anything a human isn't uniquely and solely capable of doing. Everything else is up for grabs and will soon be handled by a bot. Please, jam that in there.

Companies need to get honest. They need to prepare their employees, as best they can, for the future which will likely include not working for the company. Helping to prime the pump with new skills, a new professional focus, and solid financial planning is the best way to assure that an employee will be okay both inside and outside the company. That's true corporate empathy as I see it. Not bleeding the turnip to death then tossing it out the door once the last drop of blood has been extracted.

AND NOW...

The Juicy Shit!

STORY #1:
MONTGOMERY SECURITIES

When I first moved to San Francisco I used to frequent a local gay bar in the Castro District called "The Pendulum." It was a little seedy and rough around the edges, but it was a blast. Especially for a newbie who'd just moved in up the street. The music was always fantastic and because it was sort of the "bastard child" of all of the predominantly White, A-gay bars on the block because of its predominantly Black patrons, it was by far the freest and welcoming of the bars in the 'stro. I'd befriended a number of regulars and quickly became a regular myself. I wasn't much of a drinker, but I loved hanging out there and becoming a member of my own, gay family. I also loved playing pool with all the patrons who would offer up a game. I was a bit of a low-key pool shark having learned how to play really well at a very young age while growing up in Texas. I would often last for hours on the table defeating all challengers including the "smug fabulous" who showed up with their own fancy pool cues in fancy, oft bedazzled cases. It was always just a little more gratifying to defeat them with a janky, worn-tipped pool cue and send them packing, literally.

I remember a friend and I were talking one evening about his job. He worked for a local investment banking firm located in the historic TransAmerica pyramid in the San Francisco Financial District. He asked what I did. At the time I was singing about 4 nights a week with my band and not much else. He asked me if I knew how to type and what my typing speed was. I guessed that I still typed around 90 - 100 words per minute. I was always the fastest typist in High School and could usually bang out dictation in record time. He mentioned that his department was looking for another typist to join their team and that I should get him my resume. I did the following day. To my amazement, I received a call for an interview a couple of days after that.

I met with the Department Manager at the investment bank briefly. He was an understated, surly, "I've been here too damn long," type of man whose face resembled a grown-up Cabbage Patch Kid. He was nice enough, though. He offered me the job right on the spot. I accepted and agreed to start the following Monday.

I joined the typing pool at Montgomery Securities at the infancy of Dot Com 1.0. My primary responsibility was to retype research reports that had been copy edited by the friend who had suggested me for the job. It turned out to be non-stop typing from the moment I walked through the door until the moment I left for the day. It was tedious work, but it completely fed my insane curiosity. Reading about all of the deals in play and info about companies I'd never heard of provided me with a wealth of information that I didn't quite understand at the time, but would become vital to have learned when I subsequently moved on to a number of investment banks throughout Silicon Valley.

After working there for several months, I began to copy edit research reports as well. It was a pretty good gig. Until I fucked it up.

Every day at around 9 am and 1 pm we would hear the annoying, squeaky wheels of the mailroom cart rolling down the hallway. It would typically stop at our two supervisors' offices first and then at our bank of cubicles next, typically along the cubicle wall next to me. I never received any mail so I would usually work through the noisy interruption with zero attention given. However, one particular day I looked up and was greeted with a, "Hey." It was the mailroom guy with the most angelic face I'd ever seen on another human being framed in perfectly curly, dark brown hair and an adorable, slightly sleepy-eyed, smile that completely caught me off guard.

"Um, hi. I'm Steve."

"Oh, I'm Phoenix."

"Nice to meet you, Phoenix. See you around."

And with that, he was off. I was caught out there a bit, so I did my best to suppress the coquettish smile that had stretched across my face and quickly went back to my typing. A few seconds later I noticed the department was eerily quiet. I looked up, turned around in my chair and saw that everyone was staring at me with shit-eating grins on their faces. Even my supervisor had come out of his office and was hanging over the cubicle wall across from me.

I failed to mention that the typing pool was made up of three gay men and a straight woman with lots of cats. Even though my Supervisor was a straight, older man, he was clearly down with the gays and officially one of "the girls." The oldest, gayest member of our crew quipped:

"Oooh! Someone has an admirer."

I looked at them like they were all experiencing the effects of acid and brushed it off as happenstance. They continued to make smooching sounds and recite every juvenile courtship song they could remember about love birds in trees and shit for a number of minutes. I gave it no credence. But, admittedly, my mind was consumed by my new friend Steve.

Every day at 9 am and 1 pm I got to see Steve. He would stay a few extra seconds to shoot the shit, much to the delight of my nosey-ass workmates. Eventually, Steve slipped me a note asking me out for drinks. I happily accepted and we met up later that evening. We had a fantastic time talking and laughing and doing a lot of drinking. I mean, a lot of drinking. I am and have always been an alcohol lightweight, so it only took a few drinks before I called it quits. Luckily, I lived only a few blocks from the bar, so I invited him back to my place. I'll spare you the details, but let's just say that we became more friendly and officially more than friends.

We tried to conceal our relationship as best we could at work, but I was working with the friend who'd suggested me for the job, whom I'd met at the bar we both frequented, which also happened to be the new favorite bar of Steve and I. Anytime my friend would see us together at the bar, it was headline news at the office the following day. I've always been a relatively private person who didn't take too kindly having my business broadcast in the street. This caused a bit of tension between my friend and I whose obsession with my personal life had quickly grown from cute to annoying to downright invasive and inappropriate.

Steve, I quickly discovered, was a drunk. He was sweet as can be, but every evening of our brief relationship ended at a bar, with me dragging him to my place or his, getting him undressed and into bed and watching him pass out. After several months of this, I realized I'd had enough.

Around that time, a fair-weather friend of mine, called me up crying and asking if he could stop by my apartment to talk. I've always been the one all of my friends would come to for no-nonsense, sound advice, so I welcomed him with open arms. He came by, distraught and disheveled and proceeded to launch into a tirade about the guy he was dating. I listened for over an hour and offered up some advice. Mostly tough love as I felt he was overreacting a bit and that he might want to try a more level-headed approach to conflict resolution. He agreed and immediately called his fella, gave him my address and told him to come and collect him from my place. About 20 minutes later the buzzer rang. I walked downstairs with my friend and was introduced to the man he was dating.

"Phoenix, this is Dennis."

"It's a pleasure to meet you, Dennis. You keep an eye on this one, okay?"

"Oh, I will."

Uh oh. Dennis was beautiful. He was about 5'9". Blond hair. Piercing blue eyes. Older than what normally caught my eye. Irish by decent but he looked Nordic. And that Philly accent! With a smile that could stop traffic. I gave my friend a hug and one of those knowing looks of approval like, "Well done, Boo!" and off they went.

My friend and Dennis apparently sparred repeatedly over the next few days until my friend declared he was over Dennis. I too was

spending less and less time with Steve. I
remember walking home one night and
happened to run into Dennis who was walking
his dog. She was a gorgeous Yellow Lab named
Bear and as sweet and belly-rub friendly as can
be. I petted her and play-fought with her a little
bit, much to Dennis' delight. We chatted for
several minutes which soon stretched into a
couple of hours. He mentioned that he needed
to feed the dog and asked if I'd accompany him
back to his place several blocks away. I agreed
and we continued our spirited conversation all
the way to his apartment. He invited me inside,
quickly fed the dog and asked me if I'd eaten. I
hadn't and it was about that time. so, we
decided to grab dinner together nearby. The
fantastic conversation continued throughout
dinner. We talked about his previous marriage
(to a woman) and his, resultant, daughter. He
talked about the challenges of coming out if the
closet at such a late stage of life and feeling like
an absolute newbie in the gay community. We
talked about my crazy friend and the tumultuous
relationship they'd had, one of his first as a
newly "out" gay man. I found him fascinating and
incredibly easy to talk to.

We realized that it had gotten late, and he needed to get back to his dog. Like a gentleman, he walked me to my apartment, and I invited him up since he hadn't actually seen the inside of my apartment. We talked for several more minutes and out of the blue, he leaned in and kissed me. And it was magical. And, instantly, guilt-ridden. And hot. And wrong. All of the emotions that play in your mind when you know you're engaged in something that you can't take back and that now complicates the uncomplicated.

We realized that the blissful hours we had just spent together that culminated in that kiss clearly meant something. There was that instant attraction you have only a few times in your life that merges physical attraction, mental stimulation, and those intangible "oogy" feelings you get when you've met the one or someone damned close. Our attraction was immediate and undeniable. Dennis even admitted that he hadn't stopped thinking about me since the day he met me while collecting my friend.

I called it quits with Steve a few days later. He was devastated. Dennis officially called it quits with my friend a couple of days later as well. He told my friend that we were "in love" and thinking about moving back East to his hometown together. My friend ripped him a new one. He immediately called me and told me that he didn't blame me for what had happened. He was hurt and furious but wished me luck with "that asshole."

Dennis and I were inseparable. We spent as much time as we could together. Because of our exes we had both grown a little wary of San Francisco. He mentioned that he had been thinking about returning to Philadelphia and suggested it would be a great place to start a new family. Given my rather non-traditional childhood, the thought of someone loving me enough to want to start a family with me was music to my ears. I dug it. We scheduled a short trip to Philadelphia a few weeks later so that I could check it out before potentially making the decision to move there.

Philadelphia couldn't have been more idyllic. I remember getting out of the taxi seeing my insanely handsome, dream guy standing and chatting with the security guard in front of the hotel awaiting my arrival. It was a magical Fall evening with a chill in the air and a slight breeze that smelled of the turning leaves on the trees. He quickly ushered me upstairs, dropped off my bags, and immediately herded me downstairs for our walk to dinner. He was so proud of his city and pulled out all of the stops to get me to love it just as much as he did. And he succeeded.

He had borrowed a car from the retired parents-in-law from his previous marriage. We drove around the city so that I could get a taste of the charm, history, and architecture of Philadelphia and quickly acquaint myself. He knew I was a dancer and had even researched a couple of dance studios in the area at which he thought I might want to take classes. Ironically, the movie Philadelphia was filming at the time and we ended up watching a scene get filmed nearby where we were walking. All signs pointed to this being my next home. But not so fast.

The next morning when he went to move the car for the infamous street sweeping Nazis, he discovered that it was no longer there. He checked the signs and confirmed that he hadn't parked in a tow-away zone. Other cars were there, except ours. We quickly concluded the car had been stolen. And within a few hours, it was confirmed when the Philadelphia PD had contacted the parents-in-law to let them know that their car had been recovered in an unincorporated part of South Philly. Luckily, there was no real damage. Just a theft and joyride, likely by some under-parented kids.

So, here's the thing. I'm a big believer in Karma and those little and not-so-little signals she sends to let you know it's time to pay the piper. To have my idyllic visit interrupted by such an event felt like Karma for stealing my friend's man or, at best, for not telling him what was going on. And, sadly, it got worse.

That afternoon Dennis received a hysterical call from his ex-wife, whose parents' car we'd managed to get stolen. Not only was she pissed about the stolen car incident, but she had received an anonymous letter in the mail crafted in that "ransom note" style of gluing a bunch of disparate, hastily cut-out letters and phrases on a page to create a sinister message. The letter essentially accused Dennis of having AIDS, because he had briefly dated someone while still living in Philadelphia who ended up dying from the disease. Dennis was not HIV positive, but he may as well have been given the hysterics his ex-wife was screaming at him over the phone. The letter went on to call me out as a "husband thief" and that I probably had AIDS, too.

It was clear that my friend had a change of heart and I was now public enemy #1 and everyone with ears and eyes was going to know about it, starting with the one person who had absolutely nothing to do with any of this. Worse, he had also sent a similar letter to Dennis' teenage daughter who had misinterpreted it as I had given her father AIDS. So, she was physically ready to murder me.

My blissful trip to Philadelphia had quickly turned into a shit show of epic proportions. I was completely overwhelmed by everything that was going on and could feel myself shutting down emotionally. I just wanted to go back to San Francisco, hop up on my barstool at my favorite bar, and resume my fairly quiet, non-drama-filled life. Dennis did his best to reassure me that he would fix everything and to just be patient. He was incredibly sweet and nurturing throughout the entire ordeal which I saw as the type of protector and protection I'd longed for from my absentee father all of those years. Even with all of the turmoil we'd been pulled into, I felt that he "had me" and that we would get through this, together.

He set up a meeting with his wife and daughter at a restaurant near where they'd all lived together. It was a long drive out of Philly that was mostly silent and filled with much anxiety. When we arrived at the restaurant, he asked me to stay in the car so that he could go in and chat with his ex-wife and daughter first. He was in the restaurant for about a half-hour before he returned to the car to collect me. I couldn't help but feel like I was being led to my own slaughter but knew that he would step in if things got too intense.

I was met with looks from both his ex-wife and daughter that were equal parts confusion, disdain, and forced hospitality. He introduced me and I managed to get a, "Nice to meet you," from the ex-wife with a limp handshake. Not a word from the daughter. Just daggers being stared right through me. He went on to explain that the daughter had misunderstood her letter and that he'd cleared it up. I could tell that the daughter had spent days hating the very thought of me and that, even though she now understood I wasn't the bad guy, it was all too new to process in such a short amount of time, especially now that I was sitting right in front of her.

The meeting was painfully awkward and relatively brief. Thankfully.

"Would you mind giving us a few minutes? I need to talk to my husband privately."

Wait. Was I being dismissed like a child from an adult conversation? I looked at Dennis and he sweetly motioned that I go and wait in the car. I gathered my face together and exchanged pleasantries and went back to sit in the car. Again. It was one of the most humiliating moments of my life and I was done! I didn't need this in my life. And as much as I loved the thought of Dennis, I wanted nothing to do with this drama that was now consuming both of our lives.

About an hour later, Dennis emerged, hopped in the car and we headed back to downtown Philly. I was silent and wiping tears the entire ride and simply wanted to go home. He apologized profusely and begged that I give him time to work everything out. I don't remember much except getting to the hotel, diving into the bed and falling asleep to the sound of him apologizing and rubbing my back.

We flew home a couple of days later and managed to reconcile everything that had gone on in Philadelphia. He called my now ex-friend and they both proceeded to tear each other a new one. I too contacted him separately and suggested that I had better never see him on the street because it would be "on." Our mutual hatred of him actually brought Dennis and me closer than ever and we eventually decided to throw caution to the wind, leave San Francisco and move back to Philadelphia.

Several friends had invited me to Tahoe to hang at a huge cabin they'd rented. I invited Dennis along. Dennis and I decided to do something a little crazy and get married. Gay marriage wasn't legal then, of course. But we were caught up in the insane beauty of Lake Tahoe and finding a deep sense of triumph and "ride-or-die" bonding over the adversity we had just faced, so we decided to exchange rings. We found a jeweler in South Lake Tahoe and chose matching male wedding bands. And late one night we drove to Crystal Bay, walked down the banks overlooking the bay, and exchanged vow and rings under a perfectly clear night sky with a full moon shining idyllically from above, lighting up the lake. We set a date for the move and I returned to Montgomery Securities to give my notice.

Steve happened by my desk during one of his mail drops and noticed a framed picture of Dennis on my desk as well as the new ring adorning my finger. He leaned over, picked up the picture frame, looked at it, sat it down and looked at me with tears quickly welling in his eyes. He turned and walked away with a single word, "Wow."

My co-workers witnessed this and proceeded to chide me with labels like "heartbreaker" and "home wrecker" and "cold hearted." I felt terrible about how things had deteriorated with Steve. But they didn't have to deal with his drunk ass every single night when I just wanted to go see a movie or concert together without ending up at a bar with his friends, watching him get sloshed, and have to physically support him all the way back to one of our apartments. Nor had I let on all that I had gone through the few weeks prior with the ransom letter, AIDS accusations, and ex-wife and daughter drama.

Prior to all of this, I had become a huge distraction at work as word spread throughout the floor that I had not only dated the mailroom guy but that I had done him dirty by hooking up with my best friend's man. It put me in a spotlight I really had no desire to be in and I eventually realized it had completely tanked my respect level among my co-workers and gave anyone who had even a modicum of knowledge about my situation license to judge me. It was clear I had to leave the company. Despite meeting Dennis, I had already sealed my fate at Montgomery Securities. So, I did leave with many rock-solid lessons in tow that would change the trajectory of my professional career and personal life for decades to come.

For the record, I did move to Philadelphia with Dennis. Within a couple of months, we were plunged into their first "Worst Winter on Record." For almost a full two months the city was brought to a standstill with below zero temperatures and at least a couple of inches of ice covering every street and sidewalk. I couldn't find a job because no one was hiring in those conditions. And within weeks, the financial strain and me being homesick finally took its toll on the relationship. We broke up. What sucked is that I had no job, no money, no way to make any due to the weather, and stuck living with someone who could no longer stand me.

I remember Mariah Carey was in her prime at the time, so her songs "Hero" and "Anytime You Need a Friend" stayed on repeat as a form of coping with my shitty situation and as a form of self-soothing.

"Just hold on. There will be tomorrow. In time, you'll find a way."

Those words from "Hero" kept me from plunging into the really dark end of a growing depression. One day I remembered an old, um, "friend" in San Francisco who always seemed to show up at the right time. It's weird, but he always seemed to know when I needed someone and would magically appear and take me to dinner, or sleepover, or grab drinks and just talk for hours. I checked my pride and gave him a call.

We talked for over an hour. I told him everything that had transpired over the past several months and he didn't judge. I told him that I was stranded, and he immediately offered to wire me enough cash to purchase a plane ticket home and ship my belongings back to my parents' house. For the first time in months, I was able to exhale. Within a couple of days, I had packed up my belongings, purchased my plane ticket home, alerted my parents of my return, and broke the news to Dennis that I was moving back to San Francisco. Ironically, he broke down in tears and apologized profusely for his treatment of me and for uprooting me from my life in San Francisco. It was the first time he'd shown any emotion toward me in months and we both ended up being a sobbing, apologetic mess. We made love that night and, real talk, it was the most real, uninhibited, connected experience we'd ever had as a couple.

Still, I was outta there. Those months had taken quite a toll on me. I was mentally fragile. I had lost 25 pounds. I was depressed. And I just wanted to get back to my life as it was before I'd even met the man. And, eventually, I did.

Lessons Learned

Never dip your pen in company ink.

Someone said this to me decades ago and I didn't really give it much thought until the Steve situation happened. Office relationships are a recipe for disaster. In all my years in business I've seen only one or two succeed. The others always ended in some sort of scandal or drama and created enough of a distraction to the business that some sort of edit was issued to end the relationship voluntarily or terminate one or both of the employees.

Business has changed quite a bit since the late 1990s when Steven and I were a thing. Ironically, those changes happened as a result of Dot Com 1.0, and the whole work hard, play hard culture it created. 10- to 12-hour days, free food, and company happy hours have become the norm, which leaves little time for employees to maintain or develop a social life outside of the office. So, office romances have become a bit more common almost out of necessity and convenience. Yet, even with the best intentions and efforts to keep these relationships on the DL, they inevitably get discovered and broadcast throughout the ranks by the office gossips and bring a not-entirely-fair level of scrutiny to the couple involved. Should things go South with the relationship, it is front-page news on Slack. And that type of distraction away from the business is what calls each participant's character, judgment, professionalism, and focus into question, often resulting in someone having to leave the company and/or terminating the relationship.

In short, don't do it. It's not worth it. Unless one of you is ready to leave the company and go elsewhere. Business always prevails. Anything or anyone who distracts from it in a conspicuous enough way to attract the attention of those charged with running the business will be dealt with. Summarily.

Never sleep with your friend's ex.

You would think this would be obvious but clearly it isn't. While my friend, in this case, was a bit more fair-weather than ride-or-die, it was a massive mistake to cross that line. It ended our friendship completely and caused far more drama than it was worth. As this is a book about business, I'll save further commentary for the next book in my series, AS I SEE IT Volume II: Life. The gist, however, is to leave your friend's exes alone no matter how enticing. It rarely ends well. Ask around.

Karma has terrible timing, but amazing GPS.

I deserved everything I got in this scenario. I made some rather poor moral choices and operated completely outside the lines my grandmother and mother had set for me. And once Miss Karma gets involved you can rest assured that retribution is nigh. One of the most important lessons that stuck with me all these years after is that you must keep your nose clean by operating above board in everything you do. When you cheat or lie or cut corners you open yourself up for Karma to do a pop by and fuck your whole game up. And she will, typically when you least expect it and in the harshest most humiliating way imaginable.

I keep it real with people, especially in business. If something is amiss, you will know. If I don't like you, you will know. I don't do gossip. I detest whiners. I will leave an executive if I feel they are shady or duplicitous or straight-up strangers to telling the truth. And I can always seek solace in the knowledge that Karma is always watching and will strike with deadly accuracy. So, revenge is never something I seek. It's covered.

STORY #2: CREDIT SUISSE FIRST BOSTON TECHNOLOGY GROUP

I stayed with my parents for several weeks as I looked for a job. I quickly found one at another San Francisco investment bank, "Robertson Stephens & Co." I joined as a Desktop Publisher working on the constant flow of pitch books fueling the wildfire that had become Dot Com 1.0. It was a wild and super exciting time.

I remember meeting and becoming tennis besties with another friend from the bar I'd frequented. I'd eventually moved back to the same neighborhood and reclaimed my perch at the bar. He worked at a rival investment bank and also worked on pitch books. He mentioned that his boss was leaving his current bank and starting his own group in Menlo Park. He and a number of co-workers were going to defect and head down south. He asked me if I'd be interested in joining them. I had just gotten back from Philadelphia and declined the offer. He suggested that if I needed some extra money, they could use some help in their presentation department. He was going to be the new manager and was running shifts that lasted until midnight. I could work my regular job and swing down to Menlo Park a few days a week and work the swing shift. Given that I needed the money I agreed.

They made the move and I joined them a few weeks later. I had managed to adjust my schedule at Robertson Stephens to the earliest shift, beginning around 6:30 am which allowed me to finish up, run home, grab my car and head to Menlo Park to work at the newly formed "Deutsche Bank Technology Group."

I remember working on several pitch books. One caught the eye of the group's Managing Director, Frank Quattrone, who'd asked my friend who had worked on the book. He mentioned that it was me, but that he only had me on loan. Frank apparently loved my work as it was much more artistic and specific to each company they were pitching in both aesthetic and tone. He told my friend, "Pay him whatever he wants, but get him here full-time." And that, my friends, was that. What Frank Quattrone wanted, he typically got. Including me.

I loved working at Deutsche Bank. Dot Com 1.0 was in full swing. Deals and money were being made hand-over-fist. I was busy working on pitch book after pitch book and truly felt like my efforts were being recognized each time we landed the deal. I remember working on a pitch book for a bookstore that wanted to offer books for sale on the Internet. It seemed like a cool enough idea so I dug up whatever information I could find so that I could design something that was visually compelling. After a few weeks of pitching, I found out that the owner, Jeff Bezos, remarked about how beautifully crafted and thoughtfully designed the pitch book was and that it had ultimately landed us the role of taking Amazon.com public. Yep, you read that correctly. I designed the pitch book that helped to land Amazon.com, the online bookstore turned can't-live-without online shopping behemoth it has become. Easily one of the most important, legacy projects I've ever worked on. You're welcome.

After landing many lucrative deals the relationship between the Deutsche Bank brass and Frank Quattrone quickly went south. One day, it was announced that Frank was leaving Deutsche Bank for Credit Suisse First Boston. We were all shell shocked and wondering what to do. Several of the Junior Analysts came to our office and told us that pretty much everyone was heading to a new bank, Credit Suisse First Boston and starting a new Technology division headed by Frank. Apparently, by contract, Frank wasn't allowed to take anyone with him from Deutsche Bank. But that didn't mean we couldn't resign our positions at Deutsche and join Credit Suisse First Boston the same day. My supervisor brokered the deal. He reached out to the powers at Credit Suisse and cleared the way for his whole team to join the new firm. All but two designers came over, the others remaining and instantly getting promoted into the vacated management roles.

Credit Suisse First Boston Technology Group was a slightly tamer version of "The Wolf of Wall Street." Only slightly, though. I have never worked so hard and had so much fun at the same time. I worked on pitch books like crazy. We did some of the most lucrative, historic deals of the Dot Com 1.0 era. The money was flowing like raging rivers and the deals kept getting larger and more lucrative. We all got swept up in the insanity and it was gooooood!

One day, I was secretly approached by one of the event coordinators who'd often asked for my help designing invitations, customized wine labels, and corporate swag for the never-ending flow of events signifying yet another deal closing. Apparently, one of the other event planners had decided to become a "blogger" and was leaving the company to focus on her newfound career. Unbeknownst to me she had asked around about who could potentially replace her, and Frank actually suggested me. He liked my work. I had personal style. I was gay and fabulous. Shit, I was there. I knew nothing about event planning, but she reassured me that it was easy and that she would teach me the ropes. I talked it over with my boss and while bummed to lose his best designer he told me to jump at the opportunity. So, I did.

My learning commenced about a week later when the Head of Events and I flew to Cabo San Lucas, Mexico to do a site visit at the incredible resort "La Palmilla." This was the resort of dreams, a beautiful property that had been built in such a way where the waves crashed on the huge rocks surrounding the waterside of the hotel at all hours of the day creating the most blissful soundtrack to wake up and fall asleep to every day. I learned a ton that trip, especially how all of the smallest details, in aggregate, lend to the success of the whole event. And how details overlooked or not completed could quickly bring the entire house of cards crashing to the ground. I listened and watched intently to the negotiations she was having and the techniques she employed to get free shit thrown in or identify obvious financial exploitation hotel events managers always try to get away with. I quickly got hip to the game. We still managed to have some fun and I even managed to swim face-first into the rock wall at the infinity pool in the center of the property. Interesting way to give yourself a shiner.

We returned to the States and I got to work pulling the event together based on the conversations we'd had. I returned to the Mexican resort a few weeks later and was given full charge of the event. It was incredibly nerve-wracking, especially not really knowing exactly what I was doing, but relying on instinct, my crash course a few weeks earlier, and the fact that it was, essentially, a big ass party, something I definitely knew a thing or two about. As long as nothing major went wrong and I could keep people liquored up and fed, everything would be alright, and any small gaffs would be forgiven. We had a fantastic 4-day getaway complete with beachside dinners, day excursions, shopping trips all culminating in a huge dinner celebration with the newly merged companies enjoying a secretly planned fireworks show I'd commissioned with the merged companies' logos created in a beautifully choreographed fireworks display as part of the show. Fuckin' Mexico, man. If you've got the cash, those kids can pull off absolutely anything you want done...and do it beautifully. I received heaps of praise and kudos from both clients and the principals from Credit Suisse including Frank, who was incredibly impressed by my maiden voyage as an event planner, especially the small details that made each of the merged companies feel special. I was hooked!

I ended up throwing over 200 events and dinners in my time at Credit Suisse, easily spending millions of dollars of Credit Suisse First Boston Technology Group money during my almost 4-year stint. It was non-stop. I traveled relentlessly. And I had a blast. But I eventually burned out and decided to join one of the dot coms I would normally help to pitch or to celebrate going public with one of my events.

Lessons Learned

Murder the little details. They could become Amazon.

I still shake my head when I think that in some way, I was part of the lifecycle of Amazon. Had I phoned in that presentation or did a mediocre job of it the investment bank I worked for may not have gotten the gig. And another investment bank may have botched the IPO and Amazon may have tanked as an online bookstore and died on the vine. You just never know.

I take pride in everything I do, down to the most minute detail. Anytime I find myself dropping balls or phoning something in, it's a telltale sign that it may be time to move on. If my motivation isn't there and I feel my bar has dropped, I'm out. We innately know when we're excited and compelled to do our best work. Anytime we don't and can't reboot that desire and attention-to-detail, it's time to go. Fighting it only prolongs the misery for both you and the people on the receiving end of the lackluster work and attitude.

STORY #3: GAP, INC.

I'd landed my dream job. At least what I thought
was my dream job. I had been working as a
personal trainer and manager at a popular, super
hip gym directly across the street from the global
headquarters for Gap, Inc. I had watched the
building go up from day one and always made
time to peek in a window or through any crack I
could find during its construction to see what the
hell was coming to fruition. It was an impressive
piece of architecture complete with numerous
terraces that overlooked the beautiful San
Francisco waterfront and Bay Bridge including
"Cupid's Span," a humungous, embedded,
golden bow and arrow sculpture directly across
from the building, commissioned by Don & Doris
Fisher, GAP Inc.'s art aficionado owners. A
majority of my personal training clients were
Gap, Inc. employees who would come charging
in from across the street to hastily knock out a
personal training session with me or one of the
other personal trainers I managed as head of the
personal training department. I was always
interested in hearing about the building's
amenities and stories of what it was like to work
there. They'd show me designs of clothing that
wouldn't hit the shelves for over a year. My

clients always brought me gifts of GAP and Banana Republic clothing and every friends-and-family discount card and code imaginable. It was a pretty sweet perk, gotta admit.

I had grown sick of the smell of human sweat after working in gyms teaching aerobics and personal training in the wee hours of the morning and late into the evening for close to 11 years while simultaneously holding down a real job. I knew I wanted to make a move and I knew I wanted to work at GAP, Inc. so I set off to make that happen. I made sure my clients knew I was actively looking for a new job and regularly sent them hard and soft copies of my resume with hopes they would pay it forward. Luckily, before taking the personal training manager job, I already had tons of relevant administrative experience from my previous roles as an Executive Assistant, primarily in Investment Banking. Which came as a complete surprise to many of my clients who only knew me as a dope ass Personal Trainer and had no clue that I'd done anything else prior.

Quick digression. File this away under "finding and creating a niche for yourself and your brand." I quickly became known as the

"Spaghetti Strap Maker" by my majority-female clientele. Using only a 5lb. dumbbell I was able to help my female clients sculpt amazing arms which included a slightly pronounced "divot" at the end of the trapezius muscle and the deltoid. That's typically where the straps of a spaghetti strap dress would land. I routinely helped clients achieve that result in less than six weeks which brought a consistent procession of new, female clients to my door. Additionally, being a bit of a non-straight "leg man" I also helped my female clients create legs with the perfect amount of tone so that when they wore heels, their calf musculature always popped effortlessly without looking too masculine. My clients included the wives of many local celebrities, including the wife of a famous San Francisco Giants pitcher. Back to the story.

One day, a client came flying into my office to report that there was an opening supporting the Senior Vice President and Western Regional Manager of Gap Inc.'s Old Navy brand and that she had given my resume to the hiring manager. And, even better, they wanted to meet with me! Cue a very gay, happy dance in the middle of a sweaty-ass gym to the bewilderment and amusement of a bunch of jocks knocking out chest and back day.

The recruitment process actually went very quickly. I typically murder face-to-face interviews. I'm the type that if you can get me to the table and I can usually seal the deal. 97% success rate in a 27-year career, baby! The following week an onsite interview was scheduled, and I met with the recruiting manager for the role, a super hip, lesbian woman only slightly jaded by years as a recruiter for retail companies experiencing explosive growth. My interviews included the Assistant currently in the role who was transferring to another location, the Assistant to the President of Old Navy, the Assistant to the CEO of Gap, Inc. and, of course, my would-be Supervisor. They were all really impressed by me and quickly made the determination that I would be a perfect addition to the Gap Inc. family and Team Old Navy. Within a week I had given notice across the street at my personal training gig and was hurriedly purchasing Gap and Banana Republic clothing with the stack of discount cards and codes my clients had gifted me to build my work wardrobe. (I'm a Levi Strauss guy. More on that later.) Dream job, here I come!

My supervisor took a liking to me almost immediately. He loved to ask my opinion on things and appreciated my candor. I've never been one to sugarcoat the truth. I've always believed that if you're confident enough to ask the question, then you should be confident enough to handle the answer, good or bad. He traveled quite often and soon started asking me to travel with him so that I could get a real sense of the business and meet all of the managers in the region under him so they could get familiar with me and see me as an extension of him and first point-of-contact. In retrospect, he was actually quite ahead of his time with regard to the exec/EA relationship he was actively forging with me as his Assistant. I was more of a strategic business partner, confidant, and sounding board, who consistently got to travel throughout the region on the company dime. For an Assistant, especially at less than C-suite level, that was the holy grail.

I remember one day many months into the role we'd returned from a particularly grueling trip to Colorado. I had met all of the region's store managers and quickly familiarized myself with the inherent politics rife in retail. During a random conversation at my desk one afternoon, my supervisor asked me,

"So, what do you think about Mary?"

Mary was one of the regional managers I'd met during the trip. Admittedly when I met her, I wasn't all that impressed. Although she was nice enough, she seemed a little jaded and with that all-too-familiar know it all attitude. She was a lifer in the apparel business and didn't seem all that inspired or inspiring. I told my boss as much. And I could physically see a shift in his entire demeanor, almost as if I'd just insulted his mother. Unbeknownst to me, they were besties and had worked together at a previous company for many years. He'd hired her away from that company when he scored the role at Gap, Inc. to come and work for him and was doing his best to fast track her into a similar position that he now held.

"You're way off. You really need figure out who your allies are."

And with that, he walked away and pretty much never smiled at me again. Whoa, dude. Okay.

One day shortly thereafter we were hurriedly preparing for a trip to Southern California for a multi-store walkthrough and a round of performance evaluations. He had been rattling off a bunch of tasks to me all day and stopped by my desk to inquire about a particular one. I was confused by his question and apparently gave the wrong answer. He, then, hauled off and smacked me loudly on the back of my bald head exclaiming, "Duh!" perceiving that I wasn't comprehending what he'd asked. In front of our entire team of employees.

So, here's the thing about me. I've never been one for abject violence. Yes, I've had my fair share of arguments-turned-fisticuffs when I was a kid. But because of all the crap I'd endured with my absentee father, I had grown wary of any type of confrontation and would usually remove myself from the situation or quickly shut it down verbally or through my patented, Cancerian, ice-cold silent treatment. I have to admit, nothing prepared me for what had just happened. I, literally, wasn't sure what to do. The ex-farm boy, Black brutha in me was like, "Do I stand up and kick his fuckin' ass or would it be better to, oh, I don't know, stand up and kick his fuckin' ass?" I didn't. I believe I was in so much shock that all I could do was sit there and continue working and stewing while trying to process the flood of emotion, rage, and boiling adrenaline coursing through me. I chose to let it go, envisioning wide, horizontal prison stripes that would make me look fat as a deterrent and confirming to every racist asshole I'd ever come across that I was manifesting the destiny they'd prescribed of every Black man under 25 years old. That event stuck with me, even to this day, as the ultimate display of disrespect ever exacted on me and established the bar for the treatment that I would never accept from another human being for the rest of my life.

We boarded the plane the next day and were off to our store visits. Me a lot more quiet, withdrawn, and aloof than normal.

A few weeks later we were in the process of preparing for a huge, annual conference taking place in Anaheim near Disneyland attended by employees and managers from Old Navy stores across the nation. That same weekend I was already scheduled to play an annual team tennis tournament in West Hollywood, about 40 minutes away. I told my boss as much and mentioned that my tournament wrapped Saturday afternoon and that I would rush down to Anaheim immediately afterward to help with preparations. He seemed okay with the idea so off I went.

I played my tournament. (We won, of course!) And, as promised, I beat a path to Anaheim that evening and checked into the conference hotel. I specifically remember the desk agent mentioning that I was showing as already checked in and proceeded to hand me my room key. I assumed that the EA to the President of Old Navy who was coordinating the conference likely did this to avoid having my room in the room block reallocated by the hotel as a "no show."

I woke up early Sunday morning and headed down to the war room already frenetic with activity and filled with Assistants from my region and others from across the nation. Let's just say a very chilly breeze suddenly blew through the room as I appeared. Everyone gave me short answers or that silent, annoyed head nod to indicate, "over there" and "fuck off" simultaneously. It was quite apparent that I was being frozen out by my peers and I was clueless as to why. The Assistant I had succeeded who transferred to another region happened to be there. He, too, was a little cold toward me, but couldn't resist my charms. I pulled him aside and asked what was up and he cracked. Apparently, no one had been told that I wouldn't be at the hotel until Sunday. So, while everyone else was toiling away on Friday and Saturday getting the conference mostly set up, I was conspicuously absent. Worse, since the EA to the President of Old Navy had checked me in on Friday to not lose the room, everyone who checked for my whereabouts at the front desk assumed I was already on site and was pulling a no show for the grunt work. This misinformation would eventually become that one Jenga piece that topples the entire structure.

Within a few minutes, my boss appeared and did everything he could to avoid eye contact with me. So, I walked over to him to ask if he needed anything. He was fuming and launched into a rather audible tirade about me not being a team player, letting my co-workers down, and misusing company funds. Once again, I was blindsided! Pissed, I reminded him that I had a tennis tournament that lasted until late Saturday afternoon and that he had agreed that it would be okay to join the conference prep on Sunday. He wasn't hearing any of it and immediately went into full accusation mode that I had checked into the hotel on Friday and had been staying there, on the company dime, while everyone else was toiling away setting up the conference. Again, I reminded him that I was 40 minutes away in West Hollywood and definitely staying at a hotel there, not in Anaheim. And that I certainly wasn't driving to Anaheim each night to sleep at the hotel and then disappear. Again, he wasn't hearing it. He had drawn his conclusions and there was nothing I could say to change them.

"You need to go to every single one of your teammates who have been here slaving away for two days and apologize. I'll deal with you when we get back to the office."

And with that, he did an about face and left the room. What the whole fuck just happened?

For the next three days I busted my ass, harder than I ever had at any job before. I was determined to clear my name in any way I could and show my teammates that I wasn't this monster I was being portrayed as. But, also, to show my boss that he was wrong about me and hopefully would give me the benefit of the doubt. By the end of the conference I'd apologized to all of my teammates for the misunderstanding and had provided such great service throughout the three-day conference that a steady stream of them and numerous attendees gave glowing reviews about me to my Supervisor both in-person and via an online feedback channel reserved for employees who went above and beyond. For me, it was the ultimate "Fuck you!" to my supervisor for his ridiculous behavior toward me.

We broke the conference down in record time and I got in my car and drove the six hours back to San Francisco, mostly in disbelief of the previous several days' events.

The next day at the office I was summoned into a meeting by our team HR manager. She and I were always pretty friendly, and we really liked each other. We had similar musical tastes and she had actually seen me perform many times with my band at clubs and festivals around the city. However, this time, we clearly weren't going to be shooting the shit about Acid Jazz.

She had me close the door and take a seat. This time, she was all business. She proceeded to tell me that I was being written up and was officially under investigation for misuse of company funds for checking into and staying at the conference hotel in Anaheim for two full days and avoiding working until Sunday. I was furious. I explained the entire chain of events and even produced the receipt from the West Hollywood hotel I'd checked into that Thursday and checked out of late Saturday afternoon before heading to Anaheim. I even produced physical photos a few days later of me playing one of my tennis matches, with those little digital time and date stamps at the bottom of the photo, a thing back then. While I knew she understood, she still had to follow protocol and let me know that I had lost the faith and confidence of my Supervisor. This felt like the end of my dream job. I wasn't fired, but it doesn't take a genius to know when you're no longer welcome at the party.

My blood pressure had shot through the roof numerous times over the next day or so. And I remember getting that same, familiar tingling feeling down my left arm and that dull ache and thud in my heart that had landed me in ICU/CCU about 4 years prior while working for an investment bank I'd hated. Another reason I left banking to become a personal trainer. Less crazy. Healthier. I could tell something gnarly was going on physiologically and I decided to head to the emergency room at my nearby hospital to get checked out. Just in case.

I remember walking onto the hospital campus when my cell phone rang. It was my supervisor. He had downloaded with the HR manager and was, essentially, calling to get his last licks in. He berated me over the phone, accusing me of defrauding the company, not being a team player, and telling me that I would need to work really hard to regain his trust though he wasn't even sure that was possible. By that time my blood pressure had spiked, and I was only a few steps from walking through the door of the ER. After constantly being cut off and not allowed to speak, I simply disconnected the call. I was done. Just. Fucking. Done.

I walked in and gave the advice nurse my symptoms, which were more pronounced than ever, and was rushed to a nearby, curtained off area and was sat in a chair. She immediately took my blood pressure. Got derp face with results and took it again. This time she looked horrified. She immediately called over a physician who, then, also proceeded to take my blood pressure while asking about my symptoms. He looked equally concerned with the results.

"How old are you?"

"31."

He ordered an EKG cart over to me immediately and they proceeded to hook me up to the machine. The result came back "myocardial infarction." Suddenly, everyone sprang into action. The nurse immediately asked me for my emergency contact information. It was my mother. They called her and suggested she get there as quickly as possible. I was told that I was being admitted into the hospital. Immediately.

My mother also worked in San Francisco and took a taxi directly to the hospital. When she arrived, the nurses (now several) briefed her on my symptoms and gave her my personal effects, including my cell phone. My phone kept ringing and, eventually, my mother answered it. It was my supervisor calling to berate me even more.

There's something oddly fantastic about a mama bear protecting her cub. And there's something to be said about my mother protecting me. This poor man got the full Claire-Huxtable-Cosby-Show dressing down of his life! The kind of dressing down that makes you feel like you are the lowliest, filthiest, most unworthy piece of shit to ever walk the planet, delivered with a tone that was measured, perfectly executed, and razor-sharp. I was already being drugged to slow my heart rate and open my capillaries and shit, but I was absolutely loving what I was hearing and enjoying some delicious, well-deserved mental popcorn.

I ended up in ICU/CCU for three full days with what the earlier EKG had determined to be a heart attack brought on by the aggregate stress of the head-smacking incident, the Anaheim conference shenanigans, the HR conversation, and the phone tirade my boss had exacted as I was walking into the emergency room. It was three days of being woken up every hour, on the hour, to take my blood, wearing a boa of cords attached to electrodes all over my body, connected to a myriad of beeping machines and monitors that made getting any semblance of sleep wholly impossible. It was three days of urinating through a catheter, not good look for a 31-year-old, gay dude with vanity issues. I even got transported via ambulance to a different hospital to be in the care of another cardiologist who specialized in abnormal heart incidents and could more accurately diagnose my specific condition.

I was eventually told by the cardiologist that, luckily, I hadn't had an actual heart attack as there was no discernible damage to the heart muscle. I fell into a really rare category of people, typically highly trained athletes, with enlarged heart syndrome whose hearts' electrical systems simply go haywire under duress. Some athletes, like FloJo, drop dead. Some don't. I was an avid (and very fast) runner at the time and he encouraged me to keep it up. It had likely saved my life. But he warned that I needed to dramatically reduce my stress level, or the result next time might not be so positive.

"Quit that job. You're too young for this amount of stress. I never want to see you in here again, okay?"

"Deal."

Once I was discharged and recovering at home, I remember reaching out to the HR manager for help resolving with my mounting medical bills and collections phone calls. The claims were supposed to be filed, either with Worker's Comp or Gap, Inc.'s insurance carrier. My once friendly

HR rep inexplicably went cold and essentially gave me a phone number and an extension to an external Worker's Comp rep and wished me luck. I called it and, of course, Worker's Comp referred me back to my HR rep claiming it was the company's responsibility to pay the claim. This went on for over a month while the insurance companies blew up my phone trying to get paid for the over $130,000 of medical expenses, I'd racked up in three days in ICU and expensive ambulance rides between hospitals. I went back and forth with the insurance company and Worker's Comp for several more weeks until, finally, a resolution was reached. For most of my expenses.

I ended up quitting the job on the advice of my (insanely hot) cardiologist. I didn't sue Gap, Inc. or my Supervisor for laying hands on me or for the abject bullying he'd exacted during this entire episode. Apparently, I could have, but I didn't. I simply wanted to remove myself from that horrid situation, never to see or hear from that fucktard again, and focus on erasing every memory of my dream-job-turned-nightmare at Gap, Inc. and move on with my life. Unfortunately, that one incident set me back financially for over 10 years. I had thousands of dollars in residual medical bills that I had to pay that weren't fully covered by insurance or Worker's Comp. It took me months to recover emotionally enough to find another job, so my savings account was completely wiped out. And I eventually ended up having to file for personal bankruptcy just to stop the nasty, predatory collection calls from coming. And that bankruptcy stayed on my credit report for 10 full years. Which meant my interest rates were insane on any and all purchases I made on credit. I calculated that the 4-door Hyundai I financed cost more than a fully-equipped, top of the line, E-Class Mercedes by the time I paid it off five years later.

Lessons Learned

Never accept abuse, of any kind, on the job that impedes on your ability to do your best work.

In retrospect, the moment that man smacked me on the head, I should have done either or both of two things:

First, I should have gotten up from my seat, marched directly to HR and reported the incident. I detest the HR function with every cell in my body, mostly because of this role. (That diatribe is in an upcoming chapter. Read on.) However, this is one of those instances where I should have relented as they needed to be notified about an incident where a manager struck another employee. While it's obvious they have a responsibility to protect the company, they also have a responsibility to local government to ensure that employees are provided a safe, non-hostile work environment where physical abuse of any kind is not tolerated. This incident, had it been reported, would have been investigated, likely corroborated and actioned or compensated away accordingly. Me saying nothing allowed both my Supervisor and the company to avoid a legal battle and, likely, some sort of remuneration for my pain and suffering.

Second, I should have followed him into his office, shut the door, and exacted a little ex-East Texas farm boy learnin' on his ass to let him know, in no uncertain terms, that I would break his fucking arm and pick his ass up and throw him from his 4th story balcony if he so much as blinked incorrectly when addressing me in the future. And that I'd deny every single syllable of the conversation happening three inches from his face upon my departure from his office. And, just before leaving, remind him that he'd hit me in an open area with a number of witnesses ready to back up my story should I choose to go to HR.

Yes, option 1 is the proper course of action and the one I would suggest and espouse as a business professional. However, as a 6', 200 lb., Black, ex-fitness trainer, assaulted by some short, skinny little fucktard with a Napoleon complex, option 2 really appeals and, let's be honest, allows you to stand up for yourself, teach people how to treat you, and set very clear rules of engagement for any interaction with that individual going forward. With the added benefit of a little bit of leverage and an ace card to pull anytime the offender forgets the rules.

Judge me all you want. Business is merely an extension of High School. And sometimes you have to resort to a little low-key, behind-the-gym blackmail just to be on equal footing. I have no issue doing that, especially after the bullshit I went through as a result of letting this situation slide unchecked.

We all have those experiences in life that define us or change us in such a way that we're never the same. Even writing about this situation I can't help but think about all of the things I could have and should have done differently. I should have sued Gap, Inc. and probably would have won a huge settlement based solely on my supervisor laying hands on me. But the thought of benefitting off money essentially paid for my pain and suffering just felt dirty to me. Money has never been my primary motivation in life. If I could live in a society where money didn't even exist, I'd beat a path there. It truly is the root of all evil and robs us of our empathy and morality any time it's promised or waved in front of our faces. To me, the win was just getting away from the abusive treatment and having the clear head and heart space to audit the situation for what it was. From there I was able to establish what I would and would not accept as appropriate behavior toward me, how I would allow myself to be treated.

I won't lie. It was a devastating experience emotionally. Having someone who had been my biggest fan turn on me like that, lay hands, and vehemently accuse me of defrauding the company I'd wanted to work for more than anything is one of the most deeply disappointing professional experiences I've ever had to reconcile. It reignited all of the trust issues from my non-existent father and hardened me in a way I never wanted nor asked for.

But as I always say, "Karma has terrible timing, but incredible GPS." My fucktard supervisor, whom I'd vowed to run over if he ever had the grave misfortune in life of walking in front of my car, was summarily fired in some massive scandal at good ole Gap, Inc., much to my delighted, vindication-starved ears. That whole series of events almost took my life and negatively affected it financially and psychologically for over a decade. The bitterness has faded. The lessons were learned. But the wounded child in me still wants his head on a platter. And I use it as motivation to always prevail in every negotiation, every relationship, and every business endeavor, every day of my life. I'd still run his pathetic, scrawny-little-ass over though. Not even kidding.

Jam on the parts you know.

When I was a professional dancer, I had a hard time picking up choreography because I was a perfectionist. A dancer from my hometown dance company had scored the sweetest gig imaginable dancing right next to Michael Jackson in the Disneyland film "Captain EO." She came back to teach a masterclass and I was in it. She taught us one of the routines in the film. I was struggling to catch on the first couple of times through and she noticed. After class, she held a Q&A and I mentioned to her that I was having trouble advancing at auditions and kept freezing up during the cut rounds. She then hit me with a piece of advice that has stuck with me my entire career.

"Dude, you're a great dancer but you overthink it. Jam on the parts you know."

What she meant was that despite not knowing the routine perfectly, I shined in the parts I did know and that felt comfortable. Casting directors will forgive a gaff or two if they see promise in you and your passion is on full display.

When I worked at the gym across the street from Gap, Inc. I was by no means the greatest physical trainer on the planet or big, bulky and muscular like my peers. However, one thing I knew how to do well was to get very visible results for female clients in a ridiculously short amount of time without having them in tears or a barfing mess like many of my male training clients who, oddly, loved when I made them cry, whimper or barf. I built quite a book of consistent business by specializing in something that many people take for granted. Everyone likes to have any piece of exposed skin be admired or complimented about. My jam was arms and legs and I worked intently to create easy-to-follow exercises that yielded quick results. Aside from my pay, nothing excited me more than to have a client return from a wedding having received numerous compliments about perfect arms or calves in the dress they wore.

That experience taught me the value of specificity and capitalizing on what worked, refining it, and making it my superpower. In other words, jamming on the parts I knew vs. lamenting what I didn't.

STORY #4: LEVI STRAUSS

After the whole Gap, Inc. nightmare and the resulting bankruptcy, I was a bit of a defeated mess. My emotions were still too raw to even want to look for a job and, in all honesty, I was just sick of San Francisco. The market was still in the crapper and I really had nothing left holding me there except my parents, who were worried sick about me. So, on a whim, I decided to move to New York City. I randomly found a sublet, basement apartment in Harlem through a friend of a friend, borrowed some cash from my mother, packed on big suitcase and headed for The Big Apple, wounded but hopeful for anything other than the life I was living at the time. I stayed in New York for several months, licking my wounds, attempting forgiveness, and simply sitting and watching the world go by. Funny thing about New York City is no one gives a fuck about you. You can blend in or completely disappear and never be heard from or thought of again.

It was exactly what I needed. Complete anonymity. Time to recreate myself and exact a fresh new start. And I did.

After my self-finding mission in New York City I returned to San Francisco feeling renewed and revived. I had forgiven myself for the bankruptcy. I had written songs that were the emotional and artistic catharsis that I'd needed, and I was ready and eager to start again, this time much wiser and with more clarity than before. Yet, bearing a scar or two.

An old friend who knew I was looking for a job reached out to me and asked if I'd like to work at Levi Strauss. After the supreme bullshitery I'd endured at Gap, Inc. I was a little more than hesitant to return to Big Retail. But the thing is, Levi Strauss pretty much IS San Francisco. The company is part of San Francisco's fabric, dating back to the mid-1800s. Just like everyone in my generation had at some point owned a VW Bug, if you were a long-time San Francisco resident you likely did some time at Levi Strauss. As much as I didn't want to subject myself to another situation like at Gap, Inc. I was curious. It was a life goal to work Levi Strauss. In fact, I had been applying for jobs there for over 10 years and always got rejected because I was knee-deep in Investment Banking with zero retail experience except for a brief stint working the counter at a video rental store in my late teens. Ironically, my role at Gap, Inc. ended up being the golden ticket that scored me an interview with the temp agency that eventually got me in the door.

I remember my temp agent asking me how I fared with difficult bosses. Of course, that elicited more than a bit of side eye. I assured her that my skin was sufficiently thick after years working for the petulant, screaming, man-children of Investment Banking during the dot com heydays. She proceeded to tell me that I would be working for "a screamer" whose Assistant had taken a leave of absence. She couldn't go into exact detail, but she did her best to paint the role as a tremendous opportunity. And it was. But, no lie, I was a little concerned about what I was walking into. Given I was freshly back from NYC and needed a fucking job, like now, I made an agreement with myself to make it work and do my best to not strangle anyone or burn anything to the ground in case things went pear-shaped. I never got to meet the screamer in question ahead of time and was given the temporary job assignment immediately.

I showed up the next day and was introduced to another Assistant who happened to be work besties with the Assistant on leave for whom I was filling in. She was a nice girl. Early 30s. Chinese. Bisexual. Heavily tattooed. Motorcycle riding hipster. Funny. The type of person who befriends you a little too quickly and starts spilling all the tea about the company, what's really going on, which sample bins to dumpster dive in and build a complete, free, work wardrobe, you name it. She also warned me that my new boss was bat shit crazy and that I probably wouldn't last very long in the role or even want to. Apparently, he had fired several temps in rapid succession prior to my showing up. Oh, and that the girl I was supplanting was actually out on stress leave after years of being subjected to my new boss' demands and screaming. Great.

My first meeting with my new boss was mid-morning of my first day. In, he breezed. A short, cute, speckled Vietnamese man, rocking perfectly executed, head-to-toe Levi's, and a man bag from Céline.

"Hi. Nice to meet you. I need ten minutes then let's meet in my office, okay?"

He was the Senior Vice President of Women's Merchandising and Design. Essentially, he was responsible for a quickly burgeoning and highly profitable women's line of denim called Curve ID which revolutionized how jeans were crafted for women. To this day, they are one of the best-selling product lines for Levi's. His office was a beautifully designed masterpiece of interior design. It had furniture that no other office in the building had, clearly all purchased and installed of his own volition. His office had its own outdoor balcony with a beautiful bistro set plucked from the pages of a Parisian magazine and a view of the courtyard and the San Francisco waterfront just beyond. Everywhere you looked were elements of Paris and Italy, all places where he had either grown up (he was a French citizen) or had worked at other companies. And his office always smelled of his favorite Diptyque candles, burned religiously each day around 3 pm, much to the dismay of the fragrance sensitive, crunchy-ass, Northern California granola artist types strewn throughout the design team on his floor. And he didn't give a singular fuck. Which I absolutely adored about the man.

There's something inherently intriguing, if not a bit sexy, about someone unmistakably confident and who moves with 100% conviction in every environment or situation. That was my new boss. He actually wasn't a screamer as described. He simply had incredibly high standards and expectations of excellence for everything, down to a 30-minute calendar invite. When he didn't get what he'd been promised, he would let you know, in no uncertain terms, that you didn't deliver on your word and have no problem asking you why — often quite loudly and within earshot of anyone with a pair. Mostly in jest. I was absolutely fascinated by the man and we got off to a fantastic start.

I quickly learned his work style and began anticipating his needs, much to his delight and amazement. I made a point of learning his team and the company in finite detail and started introducing myself to everyone at the company from the gardener to the Head of IT, even the President of the Brand. Unlike Gap, Inc. I was going to make sure that I left a positive and distinct mark at Levi's and that people would know who I was. And I worked like crazy to make sure there was no room left for misinterpretation in my relationship with my new boss.

Six weeks in, my original temporary contract was up. My temp agent reminded me and was already brokering a deal to make me a floater within the organization as my reviews were stellar. My boss called me into his office late on the afternoon of my last day.

"It doesn't look like my Assistant is coming back anytime soon. I really enjoy working with you and was wondering if you'd be interested in staying a little longer?"

He mentioned he couldn't just hire me on the spot because his Assistant's job was legally protected since she was out on medical leave. But that once she returned, he would work to transfer her to another department and exec and sign me on permanently as his new Assistant. Holy shit! Of course, I agreed to stay put, which was perfect timing as an entire building of people were getting moved into the newly renovated main building across the campus. Which meant that I had to disassemble everything in that beautiful office and arrange to have it transferred to the new location.

We'd moved in and gotten settled pretty quickly. My boss, mid-move, decided that he no longer wanted an office and would, instead, post up in the long, wide corridor adjacent and allow his team to use his office as a conference room. Which meant that I had to distribute a whole lot of personally purchased furniture throughout our department, much to the chagrin of the Operations Manager who had carefully designed where every piece of furniture would go. There were some rather epic feuds between my boss and the Operations Manager who was clearly not a fan. I consumed mountains of popcorn watching it all go down at least a few times per month.

My Assistant friend who had trained me pulled me aside one day to let me know that some shit was about to hit the fan re: my boss. I was confused and got the details. Apparently, the previous Assistant and my boss' relationship had gone South after three years of working together. Admittedly, she sounded kind of incompetent and was making bonehead mistakes quite consistently. Even when I took over her desk, I could tell that she was a bit of an administrative slob. Nothing was where it should have been. Duplicates everywhere. No digital filing system. Paper files that weren't in correct order. Essentially, a hot mess. Which, over time, put her in the crosshairs of my exacting, perfectionist, highest-standards boss. She ended up leaving on stress leave. On paper, that is.

What had actually happened was that my boss' company cell phone had been malfunctioning and he'd asked her to go to the carrier store, purchase a new phone, swap out the SIM card and delete everything from the malfunctioning phone he was swapping out. My Assistant friend, who was quite tech-savvy, decided to go with her and help her out. Apparently, as they went through the phone to clear out anything of importance, they came across a number of nude photos of young, legal aged men in varying stages of undress. According to my lesbian Assistant friend the photos were "pretty hot, but shocking." And the perfect opportunity for revenge to be exacted on the screamer by a burnt-out Assistant who had been handed a golden lawsuit opportunity. And, unlike me with my Gap Inc. situation, she pounced on it. My Assistant friend helped her download and save the folders from the malfunctioning phone where the pictures were stored and reached out to an attorney for advice. It was quickly determined that she had a case and she immediately filed a claim with HR.

Unbeknownst to me when I joined the company the case was already in litigation. My boss was already under investigation and giving depositions. My Assistant friend was in constant contact with the spurned Assistant and they had already worked out an agreement to split any settlement money once everything shook out.

I remember it all came to a very abrupt end late one afternoon. I was working away at my desk. My boss had been gone for quite a while. All of a sudden, he appeared, flustered, nervous and uncharacteristically non-composed. The Operations Manager had accompanied him down to his desk and stood nearby. He quickly threw a few items in his big ass Celine bag, walked over to my desk and said,

"I have to leave right now. I'll call you in a few minutes. I may need you to bring me a few things. I'll explain later."

I wasn't sure what was going on, but I knew something was up. I'm incredibly intuitive by nature and by the way he was acting I could tell this was bad. He and the Operations Manager walked way and that was pretty much it.

I immediately received a call from the Assistant to the Brand President asking me to come and see her ASAP. I did. She asked me to draft and send out an email to our entire department requesting everyone's mandatory attendance at a meeting that would be run by the President of the Brand. The meeting was to happen in 30 minutes. Yeah. This was bad.

I rushed back and sent what would eventually be one of many "Please clear your calendars for the following meeting. Your attendance is MANDATORY!" emails. People started a procession to my desk asking if I knew what was up. My boss had apparently already reached out to one or two of his direct reports to let them know what was happening. And then the tears started flowing. He'd been fired. Summarily.

We all assembled in one of the large showrooms with news quickly spreading among the team. In walked the Brand President. For context, he was a tall, muscular, beautiful gay man who could easily be the younger, hotter brother of British actor Patrick Stewart. I remember meeting him a few times and thinking, "He could definitely get it." He had this air of confidence and no-nonsense about him that, in aggregate, made him incredibly sexy and oozing with that effortless power. No lie, I had a bit of a man crush. But I loved my boss more.

You could hear a pin drop when he walked into the room. He stepped to the front of the room flanked by my boss' threadbare direct reports and immediately burst into tears, much to the complete shock of everyone in the audience. This isn't a man who displayed much emotion. He proceeded to tell us that a complaint had been filed by my boss' previous Assistant and that an investigation had concluded that my boss was guilty of transgressing rules of conduct deemed by the Board of Directors as grounds for dismissal. He said that despite his pleas as an almost 15-year Supervisor to my boss, the Board stood by their recommendation to let him go for the good of the company. Cue gut-wrenching wailing in a room of grown-ass women and men. I didn't shed a single tear. I could only manifest fury as an emotion.

My heart was broken. I wanted this all to just go away. The one work situation where I felt so happy, appreciated, and supported was ending almost as abruptly as it had started. A team of people who had grown to love my boss and whose careers had been nurtured and had gone stratospheric because of him were now sobbing their eyes out wondering what the fuck just happened. And I couldn't help but to cut hateful eyes at my Benedict Arnold Assistant friend who had, essentially, masterminded the whole thing and would likely profit 6-digits from it while hiding her involvement. I felt disgusted to even know her and froze her out like the iceberg that took down the Titanic.

And, then, reality set in. I suddenly had no boss. And I was still, officially, a temp. During the meeting, the Brand President mentioned that the interim plan would be to have one of the Vice Presidents from Merch and Design step in for the interim. I had met her and wasn't impressed. In fact, I found her insufferable, but whatevs.

I got back to my desk and returned the call from my boss that I'd missed during the announcement of his dismissal. He asked me to grab several personal items from his desk and bring them to him at the little cafe inside Neiman Marcus where he was posted up, ironically, where his husband worked just upstairs. I remember walking in expecting him to be a puddle of tears and drinking rather poorly from a straw. Nope! He had his game face on with even a little more glee than I was used to seeing from him. I told him that we'd had the meeting and that everyone knew that he wouldn't be returning. He asked if any details were shared about why he was asked to leave and I told him no, the Brand President wasn't allowed to divulge. He seemed incredibly relieved with that news. I chose not to ask too many questions and he shared enough to confirm that I knew what was up.

"Take care of my team, okay? They need you right now. Please tell them I love them and to 'Go Forth.'"

"Go Forth" was the campaign slogan chosen for the brand. I gave him a huge hug. He wished me well and told me that he wanted me to have the two Mies van der Rohe Barcelona chairs outside his office and that he would arrange the exchange with the Operations Manager. I was too distraught to be as happy as I would normally get with news like that. But I was grateful. He knew how much I loved those chairs and it was the ultimate gesture of friendship and respect from someone whom I had renewed his faith in Assistants and someone who had renewed my faith in bosses.

It was a morose few weeks thereafter. Everyone was moving as if wading through sorghum. My interim boss was assigning things to me and micromanaging me to death. She was power-drunk within minutes of getting the news that she was now HBIC, even if on an interim basis. We could never quite get on the same page and she was apt to throw me under the bus at every possible opportunity she could. It was clear she didn't like me and was punishing me for every meeting request I pushed back on because it didn't have a purpose and critical result attached. My boss used to tell me to block 90% of her meeting requests because she was a notorious time waster. She enjoyed every minute of turning the knife and there wasn't shit I could do about it. I was at her mercy.

A couple of weeks later I got a random call from the Executive Assistant to the Brand President. She and the Brand President wanted to meet with me. Um, that's wasn't daunting at all. I sheepishly made my way upstairs and made myself known. The thing about the Assistant to the Brand President was that she was a bit of a ball buster. She was often abrupt. She struck fear into pretty much every other Assistant on campus. She was beyond dope at her job and easily one of the best Assistants I had ever come into contact with to this day. (She's now Mark Zuckerberg's Assistant. That dope.) Admittedly, she intimidated me a bit, but not to the point of being afraid of her. She quickly pulled me into a conference room. The Brand President joined us shortly afterward and she returned to her desk. He started:

"So, how are you?"

"I'm good. Admittedly a little nervous about being in this room with you right now."

He giggled. That was a first for me.

"Don't worry. It's nothing bad. I have to say you really impressed me with how you handled the situation with the team these past few weeks. You've managed to keep the team supported and everyone seems to be getting back up to speed. Everyone, including your ex-boss, speaks very highly of you and I've seen you in action. And I have to admit, I'm often jealous of your outfits. I wish I could pull off that kind of style, but I'm nowhere near as stylish as you."

Says the man whose perfect ass was made for Levi's. Eye roll.

"So, I just promoted my Assistant to a Global Project Manager. Which means I now need an Executive Assistant. I've asked around and everyone loves you. Andrea loves you. So, I was wondering if you would be interested in becoming my new Assistant? You'd assist us both as the Assistant to the Office of the President. What do you think?"

There are instances in your life where a wave of excitement so strong and powerful hits you and makes it not only difficult to contain your emotions and facial expressions but to contain your bodily functions as well. I'm pretty sure I succeeded.

"First, holy shit."

Again, he chuckled.

"I'd love to, are you kidding me?!"

"Good. That's what I was hoping you'd say. I'll give you fair warning I'm a hard one to support. So really think about it. Talk with Andrea and get a sense for the amount of work she deals with. It's a lot. And I'm a handful."

"You do remember who I used to support, right?"

This time we both chuckled.

That appointment was officially the quickest rise through the ranks of any professional at Levi Strauss & Co. No Assistant had ever gone from temp to supporting the Office of the President in six months. The daggers, nasty looks, and sabotage attempts that I received when word spread among the "lifers" that I'd been offered the job were epic. Even the interim boss I'd been assigned to did her best to sabotage the appointment claiming that she needed me in the role until a replacement to my boss had been found. Can you imagine? The PRESIDENT requests my presence and you want to overrule his edict for your own comfort? Man! She was a terrible human being. Zero love lost. And, true to form, she was always trying to score time with the Brand President which I blocked even more mightily than I did with my previous boss. Karma!

I'd settled into my new role supporting the Office of the President. Kinda. What I found was that my boss and his previous Assistant had been working together for so long that they'd developed their own verbal and non-verbal languages. He would automatically defer to her and she would, in turn, would explain what he wanted. I found this rather weird at first, then quickly quite annoying. Additionally, she was used to working alone so having to take the time to explain things to me was more of an inconvenience than she had anticipated. She would often get a little short with me if she perceived that I wasn't quite picking up as quickly as she'd hoped.

The role was pure insanity. There was so much information coming at me from every direction at all times. Levi's is a behemoth, global organization with a zillion moving pieces all flowing into that one, 3-person office. So, I was always fielding questions or creating meetings across multiple time zones every moment of the day. There were complex reports that required computations I couldn't quite grasp with the limited time and tutelage I was given. The Brand President liked things handed to him in a certain way and in a certain order that I still hadn't quite mastered, so he would constantly send me back to his previous Assistant to have her "show me."

While I was great at the interpersonal communications aspect of the role, and all external business partners loved having me as a resource, I was struggling a bit with the internal administrative component which was incredibly frustrating as I felt I wasn't being set up for success when I truly wanted to succeed. I remember one moment where the previous Assistant and I got into it. I believe I had asked her for something, and she snapped that I should already know where to find it. My frustration had peaked.

"You know what, forget it. I'll figure it out."

If I go there and go silent on you, it essentially means I'm done and will likely never ask you another question unless the building is on fire. Even then I'd feel around for the exit instead of asking you shit. I still loved the job but was starting to get the realization that it might not last very long unless the dynamic changed dramatically.

"Clearly, I said something that pissed you off. So, do you want to talk about it?"

"As a matter of fact, I do."

I got up and walked into the conference room and waited for her to join me. I proceeded to let her know that I was trying my best. That despite my best efforts I didn't feel supported and felt like I was failing the office. I felt that she either didn't like me or was jealous in some way and that our relationship was quickly going south to the point where I really didn't want to work with her anymore. Additionally, I felt the Brand President always deferring to her wasn't allowing me to learn the role, especially when she was translating everything, he said to me and she was becoming too impatient to even do that. It was a fucked-up situation that I'd walked into and I was over it. Officially.

To my surprise, it seemed to open a bit of a wound. She proceeded to tell me that before I'd started, she had been written up for creating a hostile work environment, a complaint filed by an Assistant who'd actually had the role before me. (What's with all the fuckin' secrets, people?! Damn!) She apologized and vowed to be a bit more patient with me. She also mentioned that this needed to work out or her head would be on the chopping block as the Brand President was already weary from the drama of my previous boss getting fired. I assured her I was a big boy and wouldn't run tell. I actually really liked and respected her, but she was such a bulldozer all the time that it became impossible to ask a simple question or even grab coffee together. I actually kind of felt sorry for her because no other Assistant would come near her. She had no real squad of work besties and was low-key ostracized by other employees because she was the Brand President's right-hand girl. People would come to me to avoid her, even though she was the only one who could answer their questions.

We agreed to give it a final go and things got better for the most part. Late one evening the three of us were working away on a project. The Brand President summoned us both to his stand-up desk to check-in. I was prepared with my piece. I remember him asking her a question about something and she apparently didn't have the answer he was looking for. And he tore into her. Relentlessly. And it didn't end. I went from uncomfortable to concerned to furious in a matter of about a minute. She was defending his onslaught as best she could, but eventually her voice started shaking and tears started forming and began rolling down her face. And he still didn't let up. By this time, I was looking at him like he had completely lost his fucking mind. She was starting to lose it and I turned and looked at her with a very clear and piercing gaze into her eyes and said, quite firmly, "Leave." She read it. And she did.

Our boss returned to his desk, fuming, and resumed working away. As did I, also fuming. What I had witnessed unearthed some really deep emotions of hatred similar to those I'd experienced with that fucktard at Gap, Inc. I was disgusted that someone would make another person cry, especially the one person who'd been ride-or-die with him from the jump and continue to berate her until she had to remove herself from the abuse.

We continued to work in uncomfortable silence for another a half hour.

"Phoenix, can you go find her, please?"

"Nope. She'll come back when she's ready."

"I was a little harsh, huh?'

"Actually, you were a complete asshole."

"You're right. I should apologize, huh?"

"Yep."

I was kinda done with the man at that point and was willing to go down swinging in support of my girl.

She eventually came back about an hour later and the two of them went in a conference room to talk more calmly. I stayed put in case I needed to intervene again and drag this man outside and wear him the fuck out. Luckily, calmer heads prevailed. I also convinced him to get her something really nice as an apology, which ended up being me procuring tickets to see Prince with me and one of her only work besties as a double date with her and her husband, complete with dinner and a limo to and from the concert.

That night I ended up having tremendous empathy for her. She was not only under an insane amount of pressure at work, she was also a relatively new mother. By necessity, she spent an insane amount of time at work and had essentially handed off parental duties to her husband and her mother. I remember the night of the concert we all convened at her mom's house who was going to be watching her son while we were at the concert. I remember us piling into the limo and her mother with the baby in her arms looking on in complete disapproval and saying,

"Wave goodbye to your mother and her friends."

Exacting the worst possible version of shade there is, punctuated by her son balling loudly as we drove away. Having grown up with my Grandmother essentially poisoning me against my mother who had left me in her care while she set up shop in California, I was heartbroken for my co-worker. Witnessing this obvious guilting by her mother and using her son as a pawn was absolutely heartbreaking to me. It turned what was supposed to be a celebratory evening into her constantly questioning leaving her son behind and whether she was a bad parent since she always worked late hours and should be spending this time with her son. Her husband did her best to reassure her that she (and they) needed a night out together as well and that she was a fantastic mother. But I could tell the scene in the driveway made her incredibly sad and pensive.

We eventually ended up having a fantastic time. Prince gave the show of shows and her husband shocked the hell out of me by knowing every single lyric to every B-side Prince song he surprised the sold-out crowd with in his setlist. To see a big, pasty, White boy sing every single syllable of "Soft and Wet" with me, made us instantaneous buddies! He and I bonded and sang our way through the entire setlist together. Much to my chagrin, the ladies were on their Blackberries the entire time working away. At a Prince concert! What the whole fuck was that?!

I reported back the next day to the Brand President and he thanked me for the gift idea, and I thanked him for footing the bill for it all. Our relationship quickly evolved as well. I felt like I rounded his edges a bit and brought a little fun and accessibility to the Office of the President. And he did his best to be a wingman for me anytime we had to attend events together, unsatisfied with my single relationship status. All three of us eventually clicked although the sheer volume and "always-on" nature of the role eventually took its toll on me. Having twice had stints in ICU/CCU for stress-related heart incidences, I decided it may be best to look for another role within the organization. I let them know as much and we settled on me transitioning into supporting the Senior Vice President of Marketing. Awkwardly, I had actually befriended the temporary Assistant already in the role. I met with the SVP I'd be supporting, and she confided that the temp Assistant wasn't really cutting it and that she would be stoked to have the Assistant to the President as her own. My boss brokered the deal and set the wheels in motion.

Levi's was having its very first, fully-curated presentation at New York Fashion Week. My first order of business was to jump in and help with preparations. Since I was still officially the Brand President's Assistant, I was dispatched to New York City to act as his handler as well as help my new boss and her team with preparations for the event. I sat in on all the model castings and fittings. I provided administrative support to the Brand President. And on the afternoon of the second day of our trip we all got hit with a nuclear bomb.

The Brand President had worked for Levi Strauss for over 20 years, rising through the ranks from store clerk all the way up to the brand presidency. He was being groomed by the Board for a number of years to become the CEO of all Levi Strauss & Co. the absolute pinnacle role in the organization. The Board had recommended seeing a few more people for the role, but it was common knowledge and a fore drawn conclusion that he was next in line. That afternoon, however, word came down that someone else had been chosen for the CEO of all Levi Strauss role. An external player. Some imposter from Gillette. It was announced internally and on every news station and online news platform on the Internet. And it was like the slap heard round the world.

I sought out my boss to make sure he was okay. He was as white as a ghost but, like my previous boss, did an impeccable job of maintaining his composure. We'd grown pretty close in the little time I knew him, and I can tell he was devastated. After all the work he'd done to build the brand and the obvious grooming the Board was doing and mixed messages they were sending, you could tell that he felt completely blindsided and betrayed by the company he'd bled blue for...for decades. I gave him an inappropriately long hug and could feel a couple of those tell-tale staccato inhales of someone suppressing tears. And he happily accepted it without pulling away prematurely, insisted he was fine, and told me to get back to work.

We managed to put our heads down and produce an absolutely fantastic, inaugural New York Fashion Week show. The fashion rags and editors loved the designs. I got to meet many of my favorite male and female models who walked in our clothes. We had a number of celebrities and top fashion influencers who attended the show. And I even got to hang and chat for over an hour with Maria Menounos, a long-time favorite tv personality I'd watched for years, who proudly announced that Levi's Curve IDs were the only jeans that could contain all that junk up in her trunk. The comment instantly made me think of my ex-boss who'd designed them and made me smile.

I threw an epic afterparty at a Lower East Side bar that was attended by the models, several celebrities and fashionistas, editors and even other designers and their entourages. It was an incredible night that stretched well into the next morning. I helped with breakdown the next day and got us ready to return home to San Francisco and face the music.

By the time we touched down in San Francisco, the Brand President pulled me aside to let me know that he had accepted an offer with a rival denim brand who had been courting him for years. Given that the Board had essentially given his dream job away, in the shittiest manner possible, he couldn't in good conscience stay with the brand. I completely understood and supported his decision and promised to keep it under wraps. The announcement was made to the company shortly thereafter with more tears lamenting his exit and signifying the end of an era for the company.

I dove in and supported the Senior Vice President of Marketing. She was a blast to work for. Just crazy and inappropriate enough for my liking. She would bust out a rap that she learned from her teenage sons. I would admonish her clueless use of the word, "Nigga" often buried in the lyrics. She would be embarrassed and apologize profusely...and rap around it the next time. We had a great working relationship. Her team was a bit of a hodge podge whom I mostly liked save a couple whom I deemed to be "coasting." Additionally, right before leaving the company, the Brand President had hired a CMO whom he'd poached from marketing behemoth Wieden + Kennedy, Nike's legacy "Just Do It" campaign creators. She was a very nice, brilliant woman who had loved Levi's and was a perfect addition to the family.

Her Assistant was a character. Tall, Black, gay dude who always sported a cute hat of some sort and the most dapper version of the Levi's unofficial uniform. He was insanely hilarious and unpredictable which made us fast friends. I would always laugh because the floor would be busy working away silently and would be startled awake by a randomly timed, loud-ass clap several times per day. It his way of keeping himself awake and re-energized and usually elicited a giggle from everyone who'd been startled by the sound. He was a low-key nut job. And I couldn't get enough of him.

He was often at my desk or I at his asking me how to do something or with me correcting a mistake before it got to the CMO. It became blindingly clear that he was overmatched, but I really liked him so I did whatever I could to help him succeed. Which ended up being a lot more than I'd bargained for.

One night we all decided to go out to celebrate the birthday of one of our co-workers. Also, there was a new guy who had just started at the company whom we were all a little smitten with.

He was gorgeous, super sweet, and just aloof enough to keep you guessing. So, he was definitely invited to join us for drinks.

We all convened at a new bar in the Castro that was one of the first to serve highly curated, craft cocktails utilizing "mixology." The cocktails were obscenely expensive but tasted unlike anything we'd ever experienced with essences and potions plucked right from the bartender's garden. And watching them being crafted was worth the price of admission alone. My new work bestie, a handful of co-workers and I all snagged a table and celebrated our co-worker's special day. All of a sudden, the new, hot guy tapped me on the shoulder. He showed up! The CMO's Assistant and I were overjoyed. We sat him down, liquored him up, and chatted for about an hour. He was still pretty reserved and did more listening than talking. But he had a good time and we had a good time getting to know him a bit more.

He needed to meet friends for dinner, so he beat a hasty exit. My work bestie was headed in the same direction, so he walked with. I hung out for another half hour with the birthday boy and decided to head home as well.

The next day was business as usual. Around noon I got a call from my co-worker in the President's office.

"Hey, have you seen your buddy today?"

I hadn't really noticed the CMO's Assistant was missing so I told her I'd do a search. I asked around and no one had seen him. I checked in with the CMO to see if she needed anything and she was only concerned that she hadn't seen nor heard from him all day. I told her that we had all gone out for drinks the night before and that he had left at around 7 pm along with the new employee. We both found it strange and I offered to make some phone calls. I called his cell phone and received no answer. It went directly to voicemail as if it had been switched off. Which concerned me.

I went over to the desk of the colleague who had called me and we both tried to devise a plan to find him. She, too, loved the kid and was concerned about his wellbeing. I ended up calling his phone many more times with the same result. I went to the new employee to ask if he'd seen anything weird when they left the bar together. He hadn't and mentioned that they ended up walking in different directions shortly after leaving the bar.

Fearing the worst, I compiled a list of hospitals in the area and started contacting their emergency nurses to no avail. I finally called the emergency nurse at San Francisco General Hospital and asked if by chance someone by my friend's name had been admitted.

"I can't provide you with any specific information about a patient, Sir."

"Patient? Wait. Can you at least tell me if he was admitted into your hospital? I'm really concerned about his wellbeing. His phone is off. He hasn't been at work or called in, which is not like him AT ALL. I really just need to know that he's okay. Can you please just let me know if you any have record of him being admitted?"

After a long pause, she relented:

"He was admitted around 11 pm last night. I have him listed as checking himself out against doctor's advice early this morning. Unfortunately, that's all I can tell you. And I really shouldn't have told you that. Good luck with your friend."

And she hung up.

For two full days, we heard nothing from my co-worker. I stepped in temporarily and took over his Assistant duties supporting the CMO, who was incredibly grateful and just as worried as the rest of us. I gave her all the info and promised to provide any updates when and if they came.

On day three our elusive friend showed up. As if nothing had happened. I was furious. And, strangely, he seemed less than pleased with me as well. We managed to have a brief but terse conversation about me meddling in his business and me reminding him that he was the Assistant to the CMO of a multi-billion-dollar heritage brand and that it was unacceptable to ghost on his responsibilities. And that I was concerned about him as a friend not as someone trying to put his business in the street.

I was really annoyed by the treatment I was getting and put the brakes on our friendship and providing any help to him in doing his job. He quickly started to struggle, and it became quite apparent that something else was at play here. Some minor sleuthing uncovered a drug problem that led to a bit of a bender gone wrong the evening of his disappearance. The subsequent days away were out of embarrassment and eventual culpability about his actions. He had spoken with the CMO and decided that it was best for him to leave and seek treatment. The CMO called me into her office and relayed the information that she had decided to terminate her Assistant. She'd loved how I'd stepped in during his absence and wondered if I could support both her and the SVP of Marketing. I agreed since I was already supporting her to some degree even when her Assistant was "assisting" her.

I came in like a wrecking ball. The previous Assistant, I quickly found, was a mess. Nothing was filed correctly. Nothing made sense in his records. The CMO eventually admitted that he was terrible but was so funny and well-liked that she overlooked his ineptitudes for the sake of the group's morale. I wasn't that kid. I instantly started pulling that group together, holding people to deadlines, running far more timely meetings, and pulling our admin team together weekly to discuss initiatives on the table and how we were tracking individually. Within a few short months, the department was running like clockwork. I was working on really cool projects, throwing company-wide events, managing the numerous PR agencies attempting to bleed us dry, and helping to coordinate the brand's numerous quarterly meetings and conferences we had with all of our international business partners.

I remember receiving a call one day asking for a meeting with the CMO. It was a gentleman from a company called Airbnb. "What a stupid name," is all I thought and proceeded to set up the meeting and inputting it into my boss' calendar for the next morning. I had warned her the location was in another part of town and that she would need to drive. (No Uber then, kids.)

The next morning around the time the meeting should have been taking place she called me from her car and said that no one was there. I thought I had fucked up and re-read the detailed notes I took during every call that comes in. Nope, that was the timing I had written down and that was the time I'd agreed to with the caller. She shrugged it off and told me that she was heading back and would grab me some coffee on the way in.

Furious, I called my little friend Brian (Chesky) who had called to set up the meeting. No answer, so I left a biting earful on his voicemail and asked that he call me ASAP. About 45 minutes later he called, apologizing profusely and admitting he had entered the information incorrectly into his calendar. I reminded him that my boss was the CMO of a multi-billion organization, her schedule was insane on a daily basis and that it was unacceptable having her drive all the way across town to be greeted with locked doors. He apologized, agreed, and begged for another opportunity to speak with her. I found another slot that could work where she was already offsite and could quickly drive to their offices afterward. He thanked me and promised to not be late. I jokingly threatened his life if he disappointed me again.

"What the hell is Airbnb?" I thought. I was able to find a bit of information about the company and the co-founders but waved it off as a stupid idea and led by a bunch of kids who clearly needed to buy a watch.

Levi's had been featured in a movie that year and I remember receiving an invitation on my boss' behalf to attend that year's Golden Globes as a guest of the director of the film. I love a good party. And I was really wanting to put my boss a bit more in the public eye as the marketing genius she was for the brand. So, I told her she was going and that I wouldn't take "no" for an answer. I had already established myself as that type of Assistant who runs you vs. you running them. So, she reluctantly agreed. I purchased plane tickets, coordinated with the director's admin and set the wheels in motion. One small glitch. My boss was a bit of a tomboy. She only wore t-shirts and jeans. Her hair was a little masculine in my eyes, and she was no fan of the makeup. There is no way in hell she was going to the Golden Globes, on my watch, and left to her own devices with regard to hair, makeup, and wardrobe.

I immediately went to one of our heads of design who had worked in the entertainment industry for decades. I told him about my dilemma, and he made two quick calls and scored a top makeup artist, hairdresser, and stylist in record time. I arranged for all of them to converge at a hotel room on the day of the Golden Globes and made sure that my boss and her husband were there.

They eventually landed on a beautiful, navy, cocktail length, Calvin Klein dress (NOT what I had directed, but still cute) and her hair and makeup were flawless. They ended up sitting at the table with Tina Fey and Amy Poehler and laughed the entire night away. Mission accomplished!

While she was gone, I remember getting an email request from someone at Facebook who wanted to set up a "follow-up call" with my boss. I never scheduled a call with anyone at Facebook and my boss and wondered if it was something the previous Assistant had done. I started digging through the email trail and found:

"Let's hop on a quick call to confirm your start date and tie up a few loose ends. We're excited to have you aboard."

Wait. WTF?!!

Apparently, the person sending the email wasn't aware that I would be reading the email from my boss' email address. He had simply replied with all of the information about my boss' journey to the offer stage of her new job at Facebook. Which I'd just learned about. After sending her to the Golden Globes to help boost her brand.

I was furious. That was three bosses that I loved that had left the company...and me! I immediately grabbed my laptop, went to the SVP of Marketing's office, shut the door and sat down.

"Becca's leaving."

"Are you fucking kidding me? How do you know?"

I whipped out my laptop and showed her the email I'd intercepted. The thing is, this poor woman had thrice been passed over for the CMO role. She was more than capable, but many of her (shittier) peers felt that she was too irrational or emotional to be able to take the reins. It was a cruel way to tell someone that, essentially, you'll never be good enough. (She's now the CMO of Banana Republic)

I chose to let her know because I didn't want her to be blindsided like I was. And I felt a certain sense of loyalty to her as she was a great boss who didn't deserve the treatment she was getting. She thanked me and together we began devising a plan to tell the team once the announcement was made.

On Monday morning I had arrived early. I typically got to work before everyone, and still do to this day, because I enjoy the silence and slowly hearing it escalate to mayhem over the next couple of hours. Eventually, my boss made it into the office and we immediately launched into speaking about the Golden Globes. I wanted to know everything. How was the stylist? Did you remember how I taught you to stand on the red carpet? Which celebrities did you meet? Meanwhile, inside, I was like, "Mmmm hmmm."

The day was business as usual for several hours. I prepped her for all of the day's meetings. She did ask to push the weekly team meeting, so I did. She disappeared into the HR rep's office for a while. About an hour later I got a call from that office and was asked to join them. I walked over, knocked on the closed door and my boss was sitting in a chair perpendicular to the desk looking a bit colorless. The HR rep spoke first.

"Hi Phoenix, have a seat."

I did. And immediately gave my "Whatchu talking' about, Willis" look, likely similar to anyone asked to join a meeting with their boss in the company HR rep's office. My boss spoke:

"So, I have some bad news. I've decided to leave the company."

Honey let's just say that Hollywood should have come a-calling with the performance that I gave.

It was the perfect bridge between surprise, and disappointment with a dash of congratulations topped with a healthy shake of panic. And the winner is...

We chatted for another 30 minutes about the contingency plan and the fact that I would now be supporting my previous boss, already in the know, and helping her to run the department as the interim CMO until either she was finally given the role, or a successor was found.

I eventually excused myself after giving my boss a hug. It was her last day that day so I hurriedly ordered her a cake and snacks so the team could say their goodbyes. And just as quickly as she'd appeared, she was gone.

A few weeks later my new-old boss confided in me that she didn't believe that she would ever be given the CMO role and had already started her search. She suggested that I ask around Levi's and see if there were any roles I would be interested in and she would do her best to provide a runway for me, much like the Brand President had done when I joined her.

This threw me into a panic. I literally felt like the "Angel of Death" with regard to bosses at Levi

Strauss & Co. If my new-old boss was leaving that would make four bosses who either quit or were terminated in the space of two years. While I had managed to dodge bullets, knives and the grim reaper several times and stay employed at Levi Strass & Co, I was exhausted. I was sick of having to learn new bosses. I was sick of having to send out "that email" signifying yet another round of layoffs of my friends. I was sick of walking shell-shocked members of my boss' teams to the exits like criminals. More than anything, I was sick of having to keep the secret for days often weeks knowing that a number of my friends who were single moms or had just purchased their dream homes or cars were about to be jobless in a tricky market and I couldn't say shit to at least pre-warn them.

So, I, too, started looking in earnest. And by process of elimination, I decided that I only wanted to work for Elon Musk or Jack Dorsey, people who were making big moves and having a tangible impact on the world. Enough with ass-tastic jeans. I wanted for someone who was chasing the world!

I sent out heartfelt letters to both Elon Musk and Jack Dorsey as well as applied for Executive

Assistant roles on both websites. I never heard a peep from Elon Musk (though I was up to be his Assistant at Space X years later) and Jack Dorsey from Square, not Twitter, got back to me almost immediately. I was quickly scheduled for an interview at Square. The role was a bit of a demotion and the pay was about $35,000 year less, but it was working for Jack Dorsey directly, so I jumped at the chance.

As I was about to sign the final paperwork, I was told that the role supporting Jack had been filled overnight by someone who had vacillated and finally took the leap. I was offered a role supporting the Heads of Marketing, International and the company's General Counsel. I was insanely disappointed but still saw it as both an escape from the insanity of Levi Strauss and the opportunity to join a company and a CEO that I believed in. I agreed to the position and delivered the news at Levi Strauss. I asked for no fanfare. I simply wanted to fade into the sunset and be on to my next adventure. Which I did.

Lessons Learned

Mistakes don't define you. Having the last laugh does.

One of the best lessons I ever received was bearing witness to my first boss' departure. That one mistake, along with those two fucktards aiming to take him down, took this man's livelihood away overnight and devastated the department. And everyone who was jealous or had been on the receiving end of his blatant honesty came out of the woodwork with something negative to say. And I wasn't having it. I did absolutely everything I could to assist him including meeting up and helping him pull together a presentation to a legacy Italian brand for which he was tapped to become their Head of Design. We jammed on the presentation for hours and I did my best to help him feel confident as fuck and march in that Boardroom and pitch for his life. Which he did and ultimately scored the gig.

I knew the whole firing thing had taken a toll. He was easily the most unflappable, direct, but kind person I knew, but I could tell he was masking his devastation as best he could. It was impressive to watch him pull up his bootstraps, reach out to his network, and keep it moving. The one thing no one can take away from you is the legacy you create through producing great work. Every time I walk down the street and see a curvy woman perfectly rocking a pair of the denim line he created, I smile. Because I know that despite that fatal mistake, the two crows who took him down, and the haters who tried to destroy his name after he was gone, his legacy is still intact as a big, juicy, "Fuck You!" to every last one of them. Last laugh officially his.

Manage your brand, especially in large organizations.

When I scored the gig as a contractor at Levi Strauss, my ultimate goal was to become a permanent employee in the shortest time possible. And I quickly realized that the only way to do that was to become indispensable. So, I set to learn absolutely everything I could about Levi Strauss & Co. I studied the history of Levi's and spoke to scores of legacy employees who'd worked there for 10+ years. I befriended Levi's historian who walked me through the archives and taught me more about the origin of denim than most people will ever know. I also took the time to meet and befriend everyone in Facilities, especially the Head of IT, so that I could potentially line jump the queue anytime I had an emergency. Requests for repair or service had to be submitted via a ticket due to the vastness of the organization. Anything deemed non-urgent took about two days to get rectified. Anything urgent would be handled according to perceived urgency by the people tasked with fixing it. My goal was to be firmly on the good side of those departments so that my emergencies would always take precedence. So, I constantly dispensed Starbucks cards, bottles of champagne or whiskey, free pairs of jeans, paid for lunch, and always sent heartfelt kudos and thank you notes to their supervisors to express my appreciation for the work their employees had done for me. Call it what you will, but we all love to feel appreciated and will go out of our way for someone we know appreciates us and validates our hard work on their behalf.

As each of my bosses left the company, I managed to stay employed and absorbed by another team. Because I made myself indispensable. To this day I am still being called one of the best Executive Assistants that Levi Strauss ever had, ironically, by other Executive Assistants who have worked at Levi's for decades. I made it my mission to bleed blue. I was the biggest cheerleader for the brand, rocked all of the newest styles, and proudly represented the brand visually and in casual conversation because I aligned my personal brand with theirs. My brand was about becoming a resource within the walls and having my name in every mouth that mattered. And in the relatively short time that I was there, people knew who I was.

STORY #5: SQUARE

My interview schedule at Square was aggressive. I was to meet with the Head of Marketing who would be my primary supervisor while providing support to both the Head of International and the General Counsel and their teams.

I remember sitting at a table in a small, minimally appointed conference room awaiting my first interview. First up, the General Counsel. In walks a thick, gorgeous man with curly blond hair, big blue eyes and a huge smile. He greeted me warmly and we were off to the races. We talked for exactly 30 minutes but still managed to have a fantastic conversation, even if ending abruptly. I was already kind of liking the Germanic timing and how everyone was on time from day one. Next up was the Head of International. She was a late-forties woman with blond hair whose resting bitch face game was, admittedly, pretty strong. She was nice enough, but I could already tell that she wouldn't be my fave. Zero chemistry between us. Like none. We couldn't quite sync our obvious attempts at pleasantries and I quickly surmised she neither needed nor wanted an Assistant. Oh well. Can't win them all. I was already thinking about how I would navigate around her as much as possible but concerned that we'd have words at some point.

My final interview was with my "real" boss. He showed up about 10 minutes late apologizing profusely. He was a tall, lean, insanely handsome, Latino man with a fantastic smile and a perfectly firm handshake. We began chatting away and had instant chemistry. We had both hailed from the state of Texas and I remember he asked me how I'd managed to lose "the accent." I assured him that it always came back once the alcohol started flowing but that I had actually studied my favorite news anchor, Peter Jennings, and painstakingly emulated the way he spoke every night while watching the news.

"No way! I love Peter Jennings! I used to do the same thing!"

I had to one-up that ass and mention to him a random encounter that afforded me the chance to meet and hang out with him while I was singing with my band at some socialite's wedding we'd been hired to play in The Hamptons, many years before. He was a guest, loved the band, and spent over an hour hanging with us. He was an incredibly gracious man, super down-to-earth and smoked like a fuckin' chimney, eventually to his demise.

It was clear that we had that magic. My new boss was impressed. As was I. Shit, we had the Texas connection and Peter Jennings in common. What could possibly do wrong? (Insert side eye)

I had barely made it back to my desk at Levi Strauss walking back to work when I received the email welcoming me to the Square team. Everyone was super impressed, and the decision was made to hire me almost immediately after I left the building. My first day was exactly a week and 4 days later.

I was employee #387 when I started at Square. The office was gorgeous. Very spartan and modern with long white desks everywhere and clean, simple shapes throughout. SO my style.

On an employee's first day you are ushered into a conference room that will be your home for the first several days of your employment. It's called, Square One, and it was easily the best onboarding experience I had ever had. In fact, you weren't even issued your laptop until day three which I found brilliant. The idea was deep immersion into Square culture and truly understanding the mission. I wish more companies would take Square's lead, because no one does onboarding better. Part of the first week's schedule was the Founder's Walk. New hires were to meet at the Ghandi statue on the Embarcadero, take a group photo with Jack Dorsey and then walk all the way back to the office from there, with each new employee spending a few minutes introducing themselves to Jack and asking/answering a few questions along the way. Given I had essentially stalked the man in order to get a job at Square I was super excited to get my five minutes, though I had no idea what I was going to ask him.

Full disclosure: I had something of an undeniable crush on Jack. Aside from the fact that I thought he was gorgeous in a quirky, slightly awkward billionaire kind of way, I loved his aesthetic and the way he viewed the world. I had researched him to death and though he wasn't gay, I (read: my imagination) was sure that if he were and would take a chance on non-royalty, we would be very happy together. I would keep him in stitches and laughing constantly and he would move me into his big, beautiful, perfectly appointed super modern house and force me to have dinner with his friends like Ashton Kutcher and Howard Schultz.

Let's just say I completely blew my 5 minutes with Jack. Such close proximity to my dream guy was clearly too much for me to handle.

"So, who are you?"

"I'm Phoenix Normand."

"Ah, yes. You're from Levi Strauss."

"Wow. Yes, that's me."

"Well, welcome. Great to have you on board. You're supporting Ricardo, right?"

"Yep as well as Dana and Elisa."

"Wow. That's a handful. So, do you have any questions for me?"

Wait for it.

"So, how are YOU doing?"

I could see his head tilt a little and perhaps a little discomfort creep in.

"Um, I'm good?"

"Sorry. I'm asking because I know that you're CEO of both Twitter and Square and I know how crazy busy my bosses were at Levi Strauss. I personally don't know how you do it. That's why I asked how you were doing."

He was gracious in his answer. I don't even think I'd heard a word of it. I was too distracted by my own internal dialogue screaming, "STUPID! STUPID! STUPID!" and wanting to press rewind on the whole conversation. He too was like, "Alrighty then." And my Q&A session was abruptly concluded with a cordial "Nice to meet you." I slinked back into the pack following him and watched the next newbie succeed where I'd failed.

For the first few weeks, I was pretty sure he was avoiding my creepy-ass at all costs. And I kept a really low profile. He and my main boss talked often and anytime he would come near me I would head in the other direction. I wanted him to feel that I'd had an off day when we first met and wasn't looking to wear his skin as a costume to the next Halloween party in the Castro. Eventually, we got on speaking terms, but I still could never get over my schoolgirl shyness to have any sort of deep or meaningful conversation with the man though I'm sure we would actually have had a lot to talk about, especially regarding art, minimalism and our similar tastes in fine furnishings.

I dove right in with my new bosses. My new boss made it clear that he wanted me to become his eyes and ears and help him to keep the team happy and engaged. The team was comprised of some of the most amazing designers I've had the honor of working with. Many were ex-Apple or ex-Google and were incredible at their craft. They were also very nice people which was a welcome surprise. I spent time quickly making introductions and trying to understand each team member's function. And that was only one group. I had two others I was supporting as well, a grand total of about 70 people.

The Head of International was an interesting woman. She came from PayPal and had an air about her that I couldn't quite figure out. She was nice enough but had this energy that felt like she was always too busy or completely overwhelmed. After getting one too many frowns from her when asking simple, clarifying questions, I put her on a bit of a time out. It's a superpower that EAs hold where we'll give you what you need, but you're, essentially, frozen in a block of ice and we'll treat you accordingly. I attended her meetings, took and distributed her notes, and then disappeared into thin air.

I spent a lot of time with the Legal Department. I quickly befriended these two amazing Asian women whom I loved to eat lunch with or grab coffee. Our boss, the General Counsel, was a kind, slightly dorky guy who was easily one of the smartest people I've met. And he was kind of gorgeous in a grown-up Baby Jesus kind of way. The three of us would ogle and secretly comment about his inability to find pants the appropriate length. However, he did manage to, um, fill them out more than appropriately. I leave it at that.

Square was fun, but it was intense. They had a strict policy of transparency where every meeting required notes be taken and distributed to the entire company after each meeting. This quickly turned into the bane of my existence as I was brand new, didn't really know the product or the colloquialisms and was constantly needing to ask for clarifications of the notes I'd taken. While I can appreciate the concept of transparency, this was a major pain in the ass for me as one Assistant supporting three of the largest groups in the company. I eventually spent

80% of my days in meetings taking and transcribing notes with the remainder of the day spent working through mountains of email that had accumulated while I was in meetings taking fucking notes. Within weeks I was lamenting my decision to join the company, take a $35,000 pay cut, just to become a court stenographer with the benefit of free lunch, free snacks, and super sweet healthcare.

My regular boss quickly became a ghost. This man could literally disappear into thin air. The #1 question I answered during my time at Square was, "Where's Ricardo?" It got to the point where it was the company joke. Someone would ask me the question and I'd just look at them with a wry smile and a blank look on my face. "Oh, never mind." We'd giggle and roll our eyes and go on about or business. He apparently liked to find a quiet place to ideate and would ignore my and anyone else's texts, emails and phone calls until he was ready to surface. This often resulted in me doing numerous, physical tours of the building trying to find him, especially when he was running late for meetings. It got to the point where it was ridiculous and eventually got even worse when the company moved into the huge new building it currently inhabits. The new building was almost a full city block in diameter. Having to chase my boss down in that building was at least a 20-minute exercise traversing humungous floor plates on several floors of the building. It got to a point where I just stopped. I had made a lot of sacrifices taking the role. I was sold a partnership that never materialized. Many members of the team were starting to leave for the other large startups in the area like Airbnb and Pinterest because they, too, weren't receiving any face time or professional development coaching from my boss. I would often counsel employees privately who would reach out to me asking if they should take the numerous job offers being thrown at them. While I was as loyal as I could be, these kids were young and hungry to make an impact. I felt that my boss wasn't really exhibiting the behaviors or the management ability to nurture their talents in the ways they had hoped or had been sold. Some I told to stay put. Some I told to beat it and take the opportunity to continue growing their careers with managers who would actively participate in their professional development. Most took my advice and have gone on to successfully head departments at these companies and create professional legacies of their own.

I did manage to tell my boss anytime I had intel on someone potentially departing or being courted heavily. I would schedule a meeting or a walk and talk so that he could work his magic and reel them back in whenever possible. But for those who chose to stay, quickly found out that it was business as usual and nothing had changed despite maybe getting a little bump in salary to fend off the poaching attempt.

My two male bosses eventually turned on my female boss. Apparently, she was difficult to work with and my guys deemed her incompetent. Having sat in her meetings, I was woefully underwhelmed with the way she ran them. Nothing seemed to be definitive and the team didn't feel empowered. We were in the process of expanding into Canada at the time and things didn't appear to be going all that smoothly.

I remember watching her fall into a bit of a spin. She was often overwhelmed and despite not really liking the woman, the feminist in me really wanted her to pull her shit together. Especially since I sensed my two male bosses couldn't stand her and were actively plotting her ouster. Her team had sort of excluded her from the expansion efforts and were running autonomously with only minor input from her. My two male bosses turned up the heat on her by freezing her out completely and complained to Jack incessantly. I eventually pulled a member of HR aside and told them of my concerns and suggested they step in ASAP to help her out this spin. I had seen this happen numerous times throughout my career when executives fall out of favor and begin making stupid mistakes, alienating their core allies, and reaching and scraping for what vestiges of relevance remain. Despite my best efforts, it was announced shortly thereafter that she would no longer remain with the company. My male bosses had succeeded in mean girl-ing the mean girl right out of the company, much to their delight. It was pretty ruthless, actually. I took note.

Around my one-year anniversary at Square, I knew that I was unhappy. The role hadn't developed as I'd hoped. There was no real professional development outside of the quarterly Hack Weeks we had where I learned some simple coding via Ruby on Rails and got to work on the same team who eventually built the now ubiquitous Square Cash app. While all the perks were pretty great and my new desk put me directly across from Jack Dorsey, I had grown bored with the role and sick of supporting my main boss who seemed to have zero interest in me or my professional development.

I would often return home exhausted and annoyed from all of the notetaking and chasing the ghost, and instantly head to the fridge to pop a bottle of bubbly and light one of my myriad expensive scented candles as part of my daily decompression routine. I enjoyed the amazing fragrance of the candles and how they made the whole house smell incredible and loved to dim or turn off all the lights and enjoy the simplicity and minimalism of the delicate light provided by a single candle. One evening I got one of those epiphanies that end up changing your life. Why don't I make my own candles?

With champagne in hand I watched every YouTube video I could find on the art of candle making. I eventually ended up purchasing a bunch of equipment, fragrance oils, and candle wax and spent the next several months tinkering with the alchemy of creating a really good, clean-burning candle. I was obsessed and poured every second of free time into it until I had perfected 12 fragrance profiles based on memories of places, I had either lived or traveled. I sent a ton of free candles out to my friends and acquaintances asking them to review them and post a photo of the burning candle once they'd received them. To my surprise, people complied and crafted rave reviews often remarking that my candles smelled nothing like anything they'd experienced before. Then, the orders started pouring in.

My workdays began to become a bit of a hybrid. I would do my regular job at Square but would be building boxes at my desk and running orders to the Post Office during lunch. Jack would often walk by my desk and exclaim,

"It smells so good over here!"

I knew that I was onto something. I also knew that this wasn't sustainable and that I was either going to have to quit and pursue it full time or rally help to separate it from my regular workday.

Several co-workers became clients and my candles began to appear on desks throughout the company. Square was holding its first sellers' market which would bring a select group of vendors who used the Square platform to start their own businesses. To my surprise, I was approached by the coordinator of the market asking if I would be interested in having a table to sell my candles. I confirmed that it created no conflict of interested and, of course, jumped at the chance.

I started loading up the area under my desk with candles over the days leading up to the event. On the day of the event I created a table that was beautifully spartan and mimicked the same design restraint as Square's interior design. I lined up the boxes with precision and in placed a sample candle of each fragrance on the table for potential customers to smell. I also had spray fragrances for several of the fragrance profiles mainly for people with cats and couldn't have an open flame anywhere near inquisitive paws.

The event started and I had no real expectations. I was stationed next to a vendor from whom I'd actually purchased several products online. I remember them staring over at my table quizzically almost as if to say, "Good luck with that." And then the most magical thing began to happen.

Many employees would walk by and suddenly stop and look at me.

"Wait. This is you?"

They would pick up each sample candle, smell it, and look at me like, "Whoa!" Quickly, I managed to have a steady flow of people hanging around at my table amazed that one of their own had created something that was actually quite good. They began whipping out their credit cards and purchasing two at a time. The table to my right was completely confused by my sudden popularity and was growing a bit miffed that I was killing it with sales.

Jack Dorsey had invited his parents, who were visiting, to the market and brought them by my table. He proudly introduced me as an employee and deskmate, and they all smelled through the line. It was great to meet them and to feel so special in the moment. My dream guy and my future parents-in-law at my table was pretty surreal. And proof that I was absolute fucked in the head.

My two bosses also happened by my table and were very intrigued by my presentation. My normal boss actually purchased a few of the room fragrances and later revealed that he would pour them into a room humidifier that would waft the fragrances throughout his house. For the first time in a long time I actually saw my boss. And liked my boss. Sadly, it would be short-lived.

I ended up selling everything that evening to the tune of about $3,000 worth of merchandise. NOT a bad haul at all and validation that I had something. Several months later I would be invited to participate in another market prior to Christmas that would see me sell through over $5,000 worth of merchandise. It's then I knew I needed to prepare for an exit at Square.

One day one of my work besties on the Marketing Team announced that he was leaving the company. He was a pivotal member of the team and despite my boss' best efforts he couldn't reel him back in. And it was the last straw with my boss and me. He ended up leaving me a nasty, super angry voicemail essentially accusing me of failing at my job of being his eyes and ears and blamed me for the rash of recent exits from the team. It was the type of email that definitely drew a line in the sand. It was also the type of email that puts people in jail for kicking somebody's ass. After the bullshit I had allowed at GAP Inc at the hands of a bullying exec I'd made a promise to myself that I would never allow that to happen to me again. I'm not a victim. And I would rather go to jail with my hands firmly grasped around someone's neck than to ever go through what I went through.

I immediately sent the voicemail to my HR rep and told her, "Y'all better get this man!" She filed the complaint and calmed me down as best she could. The very next morning I received a phone call from my boss pseudo apologizing for the terse voicemail but knowing full well that he was pissed now that his business was in the street. I avoided him like the plague and keep communication only through email and text.

The following week I received word that the HR rep I had filed the complaint with had been let go. And the next day, I was asked by my boss to schedule a meeting with him, the General Counsel and myself. I actually had another new boss who loved me, though using me sparingly. She was conspicuously absent from the meeting request.

I remember avoiding scheduling the meeting because my intuition told me it would be a crunchy conversation and to be honest, I didn't want to even be in the room with the dude. I eventually scheduled the meeting. I had reached out numerous times to the General Counsel begging him to just take me on full-time for the group. He and I had developed a pretty special relationship. The team loved me, and I often got called out in meetings for going above and beyond for the group. I even used to make him my "special tea" anytime he got sick. He would often text me from a meeting sweetly asking me for the "special tea." I would whip it up, dip a coffee stirrer in to make sure it was perfect, and hand deliver it into whatever meeting he happened to be in. I remember interrupting a meeting with all of my bosses, Jack, and several other C-levels to bring him his tea. I opened the door and the room fell quiet. I made my way around the table, past my regular boss, and would sit the tea in front of him with extra lemon wedges. He would thank me, and I would make my way back out of the room still looking at the faces of everyone absolutely shocked by what they had just witnessed. I'd make it about four steps outside the door closing behind me and the room burst into laughter. It was our thing. And the troops were either jealous or aghast.

The day of the meeting I asked the General Counsel whether or not he had any intel on what the meeting was about.

"Yeah. That's gonna be a tough conversation."

He didn't really say much more, so my mind began to wander. Once the meeting rolled around my intuition kind of prepared me for the worst. I decided to enable the message recording function on my phone and sneak it loosely in between a few pieces of paper before I walked in the room. I wanted to make sure that if some bullshit popped off, I had a recording of everything in case I had to sue somebody. I noticed that a newer member of the HR team was also in attendance looking incredibly uncomfortable. I knew, then, that my goose was cooked.

Sure enough, my main boss launched into my failure at helping to stem the wave of attrition that had befallen his group. He couldn't really bring up any specific failures or any administrative mistakes to justify incompetence. So, he used that as the main argument as to why

I wasn't cutting. And, of course, he suggested that my new business may have been taking up too much of my attention allowing this all to happen. And to my surprise, the General Counsel jumped on the bandwagon claiming that I had repeatedly forgotten to add a frequent traveler number to his hotel reservations. It was a number I had often told him was incomplete and that I couldn't get access to because the provider would only speak to the cardholder. That felt like the ultimate betrayal by someone whom I had hoped would protect me from a clear attempt at retaliation. I knew that it was taking a risk to report the abusive voicemail to HR. But some of the words in that email and the clear lack of self-awareness of *being* the problem was something I couldn't just take. And, sure enough, it had manifested in me clearly being fired.

I tried to plead my case, but my boss wasn't having it. They outlined a very generous severance package which included participation in an early employee stock liquidity event that would eventually net me enough money to pay off all of my bills. In a weird way it felt like the ultimate exhale. I apologized for my part in the degradation of our relationships and couldn't hold back tears. To my surprise, both guys' eyes welled up and I gave them both hugs and thanked them for the generous severance package. The HR rep walked me to my desk, collected my credit card and access key and allowed me to pack up my personal effects, and walked me to the elevator for the last time.

I wouldn't set foot back in that building for over four years when I was asked to participate on a panel of EAs as the owner/operator of MEGA University, a company I created to develop and empower the very top EAs in the world. Oh, the irony. Even more ironic, my main boss left the company later that year and the General Counsel a year and a half later after the company's IPO was completed.

Lessons Learned

Trust no one in business.

This was one of the hardest lessons for me to learn, especially as someone who is insanely optimistic and believes in the good of everyone. Everyone has their own motivations and your best interests are not always top of mind. My friend Ledisi gave me two pieces of incredible advice that I covet to this day:

People want what they want. They don't care about how you feel.

No one will ever believe in your dream as much as you do.

Nothing could be more true. When Square cut ties with me I was hurt, but not devastated. My intuition knew something was up, so my being terminated wasn't that much of a shock. What was most hurtful was that the one executive I thought had my back turned out to be the biggest turncoat of all. Sure, I was railroaded by the person who hired me. But the one I'd made my special tea for, constantly brought lunch to, and did numerous special little things for, fucked me over the worst. And it changed me. I learned that crossing that friend/boss line ends worst for the person lowest in the hierarchy. So, I no longer engage with execs in anything other than a transactional business relationship, with a friendly tone. Anything beyond that doesn't interest me as it doesn't support my goals. Familiarity is the Sirens' Song. It will woo you into letting down your guard and inevitably creates an environment where liberties can (and will) be taken. I don't allow it. Since "It's about the business" is my professional mantra I keep it as professional as possible so that the objective doesn't get diluted by emotion, familiarity, or new rules created by those you've allowed to run amok with your kindness. Fuck that. Once bitten, twice shy. And it's worked out quite well for me.

Embrace the side hustle.

The one thing that saved my ass after getting the ax (and likely a contributing factor) was that I already had a side hustle of my own, ironically, built and validated at the very company that let me go. As a result, I was able to transition immediately into it fulltime and quickly make a wage that was comparable to what I'd just given up. To this day I've always maintained a side hustle as both an additional source of income and passion project. No job working for someone else has ever given me complete satisfaction. I'm insanely creative and antsy and despite my attempts to make each role creative enough to keep my attention, I've always needed something else to provide that left/right brain balance. Side hustles that focus on right-brain activities allow me to be more productive with left-brain activities and feel much more fulfilled and complete. Plus, knowing that I am the CEO of my own business provides me a different kind of confidence making me less apt to fall victim to the boss/employee hierarchy of working for someone else. I see my bosses as peers, not as authoritarians. Perhaps that's what gets me into trouble when I refuse to willingly follow rules and norms I see as oppressive or pointless in some way. Knowing that if shit hits the fan or it's time to tap out, I have a safety net allows me to be more fearless and exploratory in my roles, especially if I can help create change that benefits everyone by taking the bullet and pushing back where others simply bend over.

STORY #6: FLIPAGRAM

I received the call that I had landed the role as Executive Assistant to the CEO of Flipagram during one of those epically gay, cinematic moments while driving top down in a convertible, cruising down Sunset Boulevard, blasting my DLR Van Halen playlist. Okay, it wasn't Madonna, so I'll retract the epically gay part. But I'll raise you the fact that it was a Volkswagen Cabriolet. About as gay a car ever conceived by human hands.

I had been waiting on a yay/nay call from the CEO for a couple of days and scrambled to turn down the music once I recognized the number on my caller ID.

"Hi Phoenix? This is Farhad. I was calling to let you know that I really enjoyed our conversation. Raffi really liked speaking with you as well. So, I'd like to offer you the job if you're still interested."

"Um, wow! Uh, you realize we've never met in person. I mean I could be an ax murderer or hideous looking or something."

He laughed and reminded me about the power of a comprehensive Google search and insider recommendations.

"So, when can you start?"

"How about tomorrow? 9 am okay?"

"Great, I'll send you the offer letter right now and I'll include my address. I'm really looking forward to working with you."

"You, too! Thanks so much for the opportunity. I'm excited to get started."

Flipagram came on the heels of one of the biggest professional disappointments of my career. After being retaliatory fired from Square, my confidence was at its lowest point in decades. I had thrown myself into NIX+BOW, my luxury, scented candle company and I was actually making quite a bit of headway. I had run a successful, but incredibly stressful, Kickstarter campaign that ended up getting over funded. I had also scored a feature on Rachel Zoe's eponymous blog THE ZOE REPORT after trolling their Twitter feed relentlessly until they asked me for samples...which I drove to the office and ended up kind of breaking into by sneaking into the building alongside the FedEx guy. In aggregate, I had more than enough money to make the move from San Francisco to Los Angeles. And had I stuck with it would probably be sitting on a very viable candle and fragrance brand. But, like so many other people who listened a little too literally to their mothers, I chickened out and decided it would be prudent to get a "real" job and relegate NIX+BOW to side hustle. The Flipagram job paid pretty well, came with benefits, and was a role that I'd essentially be allowed to create myself. I rationalized that I could do both, incredibly well, and that I'd eventually grow NIX+BOW to the point where I could work it full time without the constant fear of making rent or riding the cyclical financial waves of owning a candle company.

I drove up to the CEO's house. It was a winding, sprawling trip culminating in a cul de sac at the very top of the drive. From the street, the house looked pretty understated but very modern. I made my way to the front door and rang the doorbell. And then the nerves set in. What if this guy was a total prick or saw me and regretted his decision? He was Iranian. I was gay. Fuck! What did I just do?

He came to the door, opened it with a huge, brilliantly white smile and this energy that was equal parts dashing CEO and kind-hearted, loving father of two. I was still nervous but felt a bit more at ease than I had driving there.

He quickly got me set up at a desk across the room from him in his home office overlooking Coldwater Canyon. It was a spectacular view. He rushed to join a Skype call with the other members of the Flipagram team and saw it as a great opportunity to officially introduce me. We all exchanged pleasantries, and everyone jokingly asked, "So is he going to finally find us an office?" Everyone had been working for months via Skype and had grown weary of not having an actual office to work from.

"That would be yes. It's my first order of business, in fact."

I threw myself headlong into Flipagram. We had no benefits plan. We had no office. The app was killing it in the Apple App Store, and we had already scored $70 million in funding from some of the top venture capital firms in Silicon Valley, including a stacked Board of Directors including John Doer and Sir Michael Moritz. The stars had aligned, so it was time to become a "real" company, really quick.

I quickly knocked out all of the administrative processes including instituting a class-leading benefits plan modeled after the one I'd had at Square...but just a tad better as a "fuck you" to my lame ex-bosses. I also set up an introductory meeting with the corporate realtor that my new boss had suggested. He was also Iranian and just as kind and sweet as my boss.

I saw no less than 30 properties in an insanely short amount of time. There were a couple that I liked but were not quite right. My boss randomly suggested that I take a look at the old, vacant Tower Records Building on Sunset Boulevard. I was immediately flooded with memories of visiting that store anytime I was in Los Angeles. I harkened back to all of the gigs the band did in LA and our pilgrimages to Tower on Sunset to snag some of the cool, new euro shit that was hittin' or to discover some new music we couldn't find up north.

The realtor set up a walkthrough and I invited my boss to join us. We all met at the location and awaited the listing broker. Late as always, apparently. Easily the most successful corporate real estate broker I have ever seen. Distracted.

Rich. Inappropriate. Kinda hot. Welcome to Hollywood!

He opened the doors and we all entered. It had been stripped bare for the most part with only a few remnants of its days as one of the most important icons of the Los Angeles music scene. The floors were cement and had cracks. There were conduits everywhere that posed tripping hazards. There were cobwebs on the windows. It had only two bathrooms. The safe from Tower Records was still in a meeting room in the back of the building and no one had neither key nor combination.

I've always been a low-key corporate interior designer. In fact, one of the reasons I scored the Flipagram job was that I had successfully owned and operated my own corporate interior design firm and had relocated numerous companies and designed their interiors. As I looked around the empty space I was intrigued. It was kind of rough, but I could see the potential. I loved the industrial nature of the space. I loved the windows that flanked both Sunset Boulevard and the ones that looked out over our very own parking lot. I loved that I could create zones where employees could work and play. I loved that it was an unconventional space and there was tons of room for expansion. The only thing that gave me heart palpitations was the fact that there were only two bathrooms. TWO! We were projecting headcount to grow to between 40-50 people in a very short amount of time. We would be moving in with around 15 employees. A number that could navigate two restrooms with relative ease. But 50 people? Including women who would legally need a separate restroom? I ruled it out immediately.

After the walkthrough, my boss and I had a download. I told him about my concerns but agreed it would make quite the statement to put the very first Flipagram HQ in the Tower Records building on Sunset Boulevard. You literally couldn't get more iconic than that unless you stuck a Flipagram sign on the side of Mann's Chinese Theatre.

One of the employees at the time had suggested it many months before I'd joined the company. My boss had kind of brushed it off until he'd walked the property. Having seen it and gotten a feel for it, he was convinced that it was Flipagram's new home. I pleaded with him to let me keep looking, but he was resolute. One wrinkle. The building was in escrow with an undisclosed buyer so the listing agent told us that the owners would likely be taking over at some point and we'd need to leave. Still, my boss saw it as an opportunity to make a huge splash by moving in. We were a music-centric company with a #1 app about to move into the world-famous Tower Records Building on Sunset Boulevard. End of story. Make it happen.

Being the incredible negotiator that he is, my boss secured a "License" vs. a "Lease" that gave us a guaranteed six months in the space with the ability to negotiate for a longer term once the license expired. Knowing how disruptive company moves are I objected like crazy. But the decision was made. And once the ink was dry, I got to work.

I began researching modular furniture knowing that it would potentially need to move to a new location. Additionally, I built two large conference rooms out of sliding glass panels that provided a bit of privacy but certainly not a soundproof chamber for the myriad of nasty, contentious conference calls my boss would eventually have with executives from literally every music company with their hands out looking to be paid for all the tracks that Flipagram had allowed to be illegally uploaded into millions of its users' videos.

I worked harder than I've ever worked to get the office turnkey in record time. I had something to prove to both my new boss and to myself. I wanted him to know that I appreciated the chance he took on me and that I was exactly who I said I was. And I wanted to prove to myself that I was still a great Executive Assistant, still a dope interior designer, and this office would be one of the most beautiful, fun and functional offices anyone had ever seen. And that's what I set out to create. And eventually did.

The office was delivered turnkey in exactly 28 days just like I'd promised. My boss and the employees were blown away by the wonderland that I'd created. Easily the coolest, funnest office on The Strip complete with a ping pong table, a foos hockey table, a 50" flatscreen, big ass white bean bags, and a pair of these super cute skateboard things for transport around the mammoth office. The Los Angeles Times caught wind and asked for an interview. Ah, the retribution!

However, there was a tragic event about three weeks into my joining the company that both devastated and galvanized the team.

The employee who had originally discovered and suggested the Tower Records Building was sort of the company GoTo guy. He was a tall, sweet-natured guy who greeted me with a huge hug the second I met him. He had the kind of smile and personality that made you feel happy to be alive. I don't really remember what his official title was, but it didn't matter because he was the omniscient resource, until I showed up, of course.

I remember one evening being on Slack and seeing a message out of the corner of my eye beginning with something like, "I'm saddened to report that…" I quickly opened the rest of the message to find that my boss was reporting that our sweet, gentle, GoTo friend had been found dead by my boss. I couldn't believe what I was reading. To the point where I had to go through previous threads to see if this was some kind of joke or hazing exercise aimed at the new guy. Sadly, it wasn't. It was a suicide. By someone no one ever suspected of being depressed or in any way contemplating ending his life. He was apparently distraught over an ex he had been dating who couldn't reciprocate the same love. They had apparently gotten into an argument over the phone to the point where the ex-girlfriend had felt incredibly uneasy by the way the conversation had ended.

She called my boss who was actually driving his family back from a party they'd just attended. He could hear the concern in her voice and offered to drive by the apartment to check on him and make sure everything was cool. He arrived at the apartment and knocked on the front door. He didn't receive an answer but noticed a light on in the apartment and music softly playing, so he walked around the side of the house to peek through a window. And that's when he discovered his dear friend slumped on the couch. It was a typical, warm LA evening so the window was cracked. He managed to hurriedly open the window and climb into the apartment. He rushed to his friend but found that his body was already cold and that there was nothing he or anyone could do to revive him at that point. He was gone. He returned to the car where his wife and child were to deliver the terrible news and called for the paramedics and coroner.

This was all delivered the following morning on the most gut-wrenching conference call I have ever witnessed in my life. This strong, charismatic, testosterone-filled man, who had quickly established himself to me as one of the strongest people I knew, who only a six months prior delivered his own son when the midwife got stuck in notoriously bad LA traffic, was reduced to a audibly sobbing, heartbroken, shell of himself trying to keep it together enough to at least tell the story. I walked over to him and just placed my hand on his back. For the first time in my life, I didn't know what to do or how to comfort someone. So, I just let him know that I was there hoping it would provide some comfort during his unspeakable grief.

The company essentially stopped cold for about two weeks. Everyone on the conference call was sobbing, devastated and heartbroken. The newer employees like me and a couple of others who didn't know the deceased employee very well simply allowed our teammates to grieve and did our best to keep the train on the tracks. My boss would intermittently burst into tears for about a week after the tragedy. His wife, who was best friends with the deceased, had the roughest time of all. He was her confidant and unofficial godfather to her children. She was inconsolable, which ironically helped pull my boss out of his grief to help her with hers.

I jumped in to help with cremation arrangements and preparations for the memorial service. Arrangements were made to bring the deceased's mother from Iran to the States. One huge point of contention was that the family didn't want to tell their mother that her son was deceased. Despite my pleas for them to tell her, which I found incredibly cruel and heartless, the family chose not to tell her until she had arrived in the States. Let's just say that didn't go over quite how they may have planned.

I remember her essentially being carried into the memorial looking distraught, exhausted and likely medicated to deal with her unbearable grief. It was heartbreaking to witness, despite one of the most beautiful and moving memorials I've ever attended. His life was celebrated that night, not mourned. And I vowed that the Flipagram office in the location he had envisioned would be the ultimate homage to his memory. And I believe I succeeded in making him proud. My boss created a permanent, posthumous role called the Chief Intangibles

Officer where he advised us daily from the other side. And to this day, there may or may not be a permanent, hidden memorial to him woven into the fabric of that building that will stand as long as the building does. I'll never tell.

One of the things that I loved about the Flipagram role was that I was in a constant state of being in over my head. At least by perception. No way I should have had mostly unchallenged access to $70 million dollars in funding. No way I should have been the Interim Controller for the company for the entire time I was employed there. And at no time did my inexperience (on paper) become more evident than when dealing with the construction community of Los Angeles. I was often flabbergasted by the tardiness, over-inflated egos and decent-at-best work that I was seeing. I remember hiring the general contractor for the light refresh of the interior of the Tower Records building. It was clearly not a full remodel or anything all that noteworthy. What it was, however, was an audition for the space I'd planned to build out after the License expired and we were on to the next location.

I remember the General Contractor being nice enough, but clearly "that guy." The one who'd done one or two big, noteworthy projects many years prior that he was trading on like they were his Taj Mahal or some shit. They were cute. But not all that imaginative. But since he came highly recommended and I was on a tight timeline, I took the chance. Once the ink was dry, I never really saw the man again. Only his subcontractors, which I had to run, and project manage most of the time myself. I remember growing increasingly frustrated that the project was moving so slowly. One incident in particular pretty much sealed the fate of this particular GC at the hands of one of his subs. I had asked for a frameless, seamless whiteboard be installed in one of my conference rooms. Because of the size of the wall I had to special order the whiteboards which arrived fully assembled and on a pallet. We realized that they'd have to be disassembled and mounted side by side with a seam running down the middle of them both. Any normal human being would assume that an effort would be made to either camouflage the seam or to make it somehow useable given the purpose of a whiteboard. Nope. They installed them with the exposed seam and, worse, measured from the center of the wall vs. the visual center of the room. How do you not know this?

One thing I teach is that the small details are always what you're judged most critically on. The installed board looked sloppy, wasn't centered and reflected poorly on me. NOT cool. To add insult to injury, the subcontractor that was hired for my job was a curmudgeon of epic proportions. Bitching from the second he walked through the door. He was furious that he had to disassemble the delivered boards and that no one told him that's what he'd be working on. As he was measuring from the center of the room, I suggested he work from the visual center as that's where the eye would go. He didn't listen and fought me the entire time until I relented. Lesson learned. And to make it worse, I overheard him mumbling, "I didn't want to do this fucking job in the first place. Why am I even doing this bullshit?" I almost lost it. Especially since my project was already flirting with being a week behind, I had paid a premium for sloppy work, and now I have some disgruntled motherfucker in my office complaining about having to do work he should be grateful to have.

Needless to say, I got the General Contractor on the phone and insisted in no uncertain terms that he beat a path to my office ASAP. My mother was a debate champ in school. She was relentless as I grew up which led to many spirited arguments between Aries mom and Cancer child. When the GC showed up, I can definitely confirm that we turn into our parents at some point. I let him have it, with facts and figures. I showed him the sloppy work that had been done by his subcontractor. I reminded him of the scope of work that still hadn't been completed and was about to be pulled and reassigned. I even suggested that he was coasting on my project and reminded him that we'd be moving in six short months and I had millions of dollars at my disposal to build out our next office and that he was likely no longer in the running. His condescending attitude toward me, an Assistant, finally came to a head.

"I've worked on some of the biggest projects in Los Angeles County. I've gotten tons of press and awards for my work."

"I've seen your work and to be honest with you I'm not that impressed."

Ooooh, Phoenix! You went there. This man turned a shade of hatred red that I wish I could color match to paint one of my rooms. It was funny to watch someone so full of themselves that he had to quickly navigate between being offended and disrespected at the hands of this Black, gay, Assistant who was clearly out of his league. But what I've learned working for some of the best and brightest CEOs is that the customer truly is always right and can fire you one moment and be on the phone preparing the lawsuit to recoup funds the next.

Luckily, my realtor was there and stepped in just in time. He calmed us both down and we did a thorough walkthrough of the work that was done and what was still pending. We set new timelines and the GC promised to spend more time at the site to assure that It was completed. And he kept his promise. The work was completed rapidly and perfectly. I paid him his money and immediately scratched his name from the list of potential GCs for the new office project.

This harkens back to the chapter about my father. If I feel that you are deceiving me, offering placations instead of results, or in anyway not living up to the expectation that you'd set willingly, you're dead to me. Just like my father. That experience cemented who I am as a person and what I will and will not take as treatment by another human being. When I said that, "People, essentially, do not change," this is case in point. It would be a cold day in hell to find me relenting on how I allow myself to be treated. I can readily admit that this is one stance I won't change, even to the detriment of my own growth.

Simultaneously, I was dealing with The City of West Hollywood. My boss tasked me with not only painting the building Flipagram red, this gaudy, bright red-orange color that was impossible to match, but he wanted adorn the exterior with matching 6-foot circumference lighted logos that mimicked those Viewmaster wheels with the tiny picture windows along the outer edge of the wheels viewed through the goggle looking contraption we all had as children of the 60s and 70s. Given that we were inhabiting the old Tower Records space, I thought we'd have no issue erecting the signs and went about getting them made. Boy, was I wrong. I mocked up not only the signs but a finished rendering of the exterior of the building once the painting was done and the signage was erected and took it to The City to get approval. I remember having a meeting with a Junior City Planner and his boss. They both loved the designs and wanted to do something even more elaborate like adding glamour graffiti by Shepard Fairey on the exterior of the building as part of a City-led artist collaboration initiative. While I appreciated their interested in the design of my office, I shut that shit down with a quickness and mentioned that I had a 30-foot interior wall that he would be welcome to. The nerve! They both reacted in that slightly disappointed, "this would have been really cool," kind of way, but I could give two fucks. Can you approve this hideous paint job and my signs, please? That's why I'm here.

I got verbal approval at that meeting, but they wanted some specific info about the signs from the sign maker himself. Luckily the vendor I had chosen had worked all over West Hollywood including some of the most iconic signs in the region. He ended up making a few trips to The City to get the signs approved. And failed. I received a call from the Junior Planner essentially reneging on the verbal approval I'd received just days before. I questioned what the issue was, and he had concerns that the sign would be too distracting because of the size of the wheels. Of course, I had to remind him that this was the motherfucking Tower Records Building that had an 18-foot Godzilla on top of the structure for months, that had hand painted album covers of new releases slapped on the side of the building the entire time and some sort of ridiculous advertising campaign screaming "Stop Your Car and Get Your Ass in Here!" He wasn't having it. He felt that in some way it didn't go with the character of the surrounding buildings. Lie. I drove down the Strip late one night and measured the humungous round sign adorning the outside of The Comedy Story. The circumference of that sign was 30% larger than the sign I was proposing. He proceeded to recite some lame-ass grandfather clause, which I quickly refuted as a double standard. I could tell by the shitty, condescending tone of his voice that he was on my team, if you know what I mean. And that this cockblockage was his chess move as a fellow alpha.

One of the most important lessons I learned from Empress Oprah Winfrey herself was, "Never walk over someone. Simply go around." It was clear that this guy had it out for me. Not even sure why. Didn't even care. I had a directive from my boss to hurry up and get those signs up even before we moved into office. And that's what I planned to do. Since I was at a dead end with The City, I tried to figure out what "going around" would look like. I researched all of the Junior Planner's superiors and remembered that one was in the room. I emailed her to let her know what the Junior Planner had decreed and found out that he'd essentially lied and blamed the permit rejection on her. VERY interesting. Out of loyalty, clearly, she chose to let the ruling stand and suggested I reduce the size of the signs and only have them on one side of the building vs. two or only use the word mark and not the big, lighted wheels. To which I flashed double bananas. It quickly became clear that my only recourse was to go above everyone's head. So, I emailed the mayor.

Writing has always been a strength throughout my career. Especially writing compelling business content. I wrote an impassioned letter to the Mayor of West Hollywood introducing him to my boss, reminding him of the $70 million dollars in funding our music and video app had secured, and that we had specifically chosen to take up residence in that iconic building because we wanted to bring a similar spirit back to what I deemed "The Silicon Strip" with numerous other newly funded startups in the area like Tinder and College Humor. I told him about the difficulty I was having with The City regarding erecting our signage and implored of him to help in any way he could. My suggestion was that he meet my boss for lunch and get the story first hand.

The Mayor himself replied almost immediately and set up a time to meet with my boss.

I had been telling my boss all of the trouble I was having. I can tell he was pretty impressed that I had scored the lunch with the Mayor. They met at the SoHo House and apparently had a fantastic lunch. I knew that if I could get my boss in front of the Mayor it was a done deal. And, sure enough, it was. The Mayor wrote me to tell me that he had spoken to his people at The City and granted the necessary approvals. And I received the very best present I could ever have gotten. I had to meet once more with the cockblocking Junior City Planner to sign off on all of my documentation. Oh, to be a fly on the wall at that little encounter. The shade being thrown from both of us, especially me, the victorious, who had snatched his balls and made a pair of really ugly earrings I'd never wear. He managed to muster a fake ass smile, sign and stamp my paperwork and send me to the accountant who was waiting with bells on. The entire transaction took about 10 minutes whereas I had wasted full-on days at The City trying to get the signs approved.

We painted the building Flipagram red first. It was hideous. But it was effective. Watching the "WTF?!" faces of people walking and driving by was worth the price of admission alone. I entertained a steady stream of visitors popping into the building asking, "What is this?" The day my signs arrived I knew shit had gotten real. They went up quickly and contrasted the foul color of the building perfectly. They were big, bright and statement making. And they represented both my personal triumph over adversity and completion of the homage I was creating for our deceased employee. I have never been prouder of myself for seeing something through to the end even when faced with what some would consider insurmountable odds. And for that Junior City Planner...fuck that guy!

Lessons Learned

Wait for no one. Go around.

This role, more than any, taught me the power of going around. Oprah once said, "Never walk over people. Go around." It's one of those golden nuggets that stuck with me. I tend to work in hyper speed and am continuously disappointed by the human race, especially those charged with customer service and who move at snail's pace or use what modicum of power they have to cockblock someone else's progress. Anytime I don't get what I'm after and have made every attempt to follow the rules, I'm already on the org chart looking for the next two people up the chain from whom I'm dealing with. It's not to cause drama, it's to get shit done.

Too often we remain beholden to the whims and schedules of others without seeking an alternative path to a desired result. Time gets wasted. People get frustrated. And if you're in a service role, your credibility can get tanked by someone who isn't being held to the same timeline or standard. My brand means everything to me, and I protect it with my life. If anything threatens to denigrate my brand you can bet your ass it's game on. I'll be on the phone to your boss and your boss' boss to make sure everyone knows what I'm trying to achieve, the difficulty I'm experiencing, and together create some sort of game plan and resolution to achieve my desired result. No harm done except maybe a bruised ego or two. And I'm off to the next fire.

When given the opportunity and support, people will shine.

One reason my boss at Flipagram will always be a deity in my life is that he believed in me. And gave me the opportunity to spread my wings as far and wide as I could stretch them. Sure, he had to reel me in a bit from time-to-time, but he had displayed a type of faith in me that I often didn't have in myself. Given the insane amount of responsibility that I chose to take on I should have failed. But the fact that he provided the opportunity for me to try and offered advice and course corrections along the way allowed me to grow exponentially as a professional. By the end of that role I had a level of self-confidence that no one could rival.

People will succeed when given the opportunity and support to do so. They rarely will when micro-managed or given tasks with zero direction, impossible deadlines, and no support. It's important to set people up for success and provide just enough direction and support to confidently swan dive from the nest. That consistent 10 or 15 minutes to check-in, provide feedback or course corrections, can be exactly what someone needs to succeed wildly. Without it and some feeling of support toward reaching the goal, you invite in many factors that have nothing to do with business like abandonment issues, previous bad experiences, doubt, fear of failure or disappointment, and a host of gnarly emotions that distract from achieving the objective. Take the time to be present even in small doses. The ROI is so much more than you can imagine.

STORY #7: THE AR HELMET COMPANY NIGHTMARE

I had gotten engaged to one of my best friends on November 1, 2015. It was a day I never thought would happen, especially with someone whom I had known and loved for 17 years but could never seem to find myself single at a time when he was as well. Magically, the serendipity finally happened and we both decided to leap at the opportunity before it disappeared again.

Unbeknownst to me, he had orchestrated the perfect beachside proposal in his hometown of Santa Barbara, California. Well, sort of. I remember being at work one day and fielding an email. It was my soon-to-be-fiancé asking for my hat size as well as requesting that I trace my left and right hands. Odd requests for sure which immediately makes an Executive Assistant suspicious. I complied but was too busy at that time to think too much about it.

He flew down to LA for Halloween and brought pirate costumes. That explained the hat size question. We hadn't seen each other in a while so it was good to hang out and get reacquainted. We loaded the car the next day and made the drive to Santa Barbara, a location we'd both decided on for a little getaway. He was raised there and wanted to show me his hometown. I'd heard that it was beautiful and since I'd never been it sounded like the perfect place.

When we arrived in town, he took the driver's seat and gave me a mini tour of all of his childhood haunts, including the two houses where he grew up. We even drove past Oprah Winfrey's estate marveling at the beautiful fence out front. That's about all you're going see of Oprah's estate, honey, unless you get a special invitation.

As we were driving alongside the water, we decided to stop at an art walk that stretched along the sidewalk near the street. There were scores of tables and booths of some really good artisans showing their wares. I ended up purchasing a beautiful sterling silver link bracelet from one artisan as well as a beautiful camphor wood bowl that I covet to this day. We left there to check into the hotel, drop our bags and find something to eat, STAT. When I get hungry, let's just say, I'm a far less pleasant version of myself.

We dropped our bags and headed out. Just as we were getting onto the elevator a room service attendant swept past us with a bottle of Veuve

Clicquot in a beautiful sterling silver ice bucket. I can spot that orange label anywhere.

"Somebody's getting lucky tonight!" I remarked. That's my favorite champagne and I couldn't wait to get some food in me and wash it down with some bubbly of our own at whatever restaurant we ended up at.

Walter suggested we walk across the street to the beach and quickly check it out. I was wearing a $500 pair of shoes from my favorite bespoke, Australian cobbler and was annoyed that I had to take them off to get sand in between my toes. But he was adamant, so I complied. We walked to the end of this short stretch of beach, took some short iPhone videos of birds frolicking in the water and a couple of selfies. We started heading back because the murderous feelings being stirred up from the lack of food in my belly were gathering like rain clouds. Walter had stopped behind me looking at what appeared to be the remnants of a sandcastle. I was annoyed by this point and was beating a path back to pavement to get the sand off my feet as best I could and head to the restaurant, STAT.

"Hey, Phoenix!"

I turned around to see what the hell he was so enamored with and there he was. On one knee, with a bright blue Tiffany box popped open exposing a beautiful silver band ring.

"Will you marry me?"

Just so we're clear, I'm a terrible human being. I was so shocked by the gesture I wasn't sure how to react. We were on a crowded beach in a town I knew nothing about. It was hot as hell and I wearing all black clothing. And I was starving. As an admitted control freak, I despise surprises so being proposed to by someone I had loved for almost two decades whom I never thought would love me this much to want to marry me, was a bit too much to process in-the-moment. I wanted to cry. I wanted to run to him and be swung around in a circle like those cheesy commercials that made me tear up for years. Instead...

"Oh my God, GET UP!"

My newly betrothed was visibly confused.

"GET UP!"

He stood up and scrambled over to me. I gave him a huge hug and as demure a kiss as two dudes on a crowded beach could get away with without an angry flip flop being hurled in our direction. He slid the ring onto my finger. It fit perfectly. I instantly recalled the clumsy hand tracing request. Well played, bruh, albeit not very subtle.

Ironically, there was a lesbian couple chilling nearby, sunbathing topless (awkward!) whom we asked to take a photo of us to mark the special occasion. They were super sweet and congratulated us on the engagement they had just witnessed. We walked back to street, dusted off our feet, and headed back to the hotel so that I could change shoes. We walked into the room and sitting on the desk was the bottle of Veuve Clicquot in the beautiful ice bucket I had earlier seen coming out of the elevator, much to the delight of my newly betrothed.

"Man, that was close! If we'd left the room even a few seconds later, he would have blown the surprise."

I had to giggle. Especially given that I'd coordinated things like that for my bosses on a daily basis. I was really impressed by the effort and was finally feeling over the moon at the fact that I had just been proposed to. On a beach in

Santa Barbara on a perfectly clear day. I was about to get married to my best friend and I couldn't be happier.

I took that moment to retrieve a little box of my own from my bag. Unbeknownst to anyone, I, too, was planning to propose that weekend. I had researched rings for about a month and had chosen this beautiful mixed media ring made of a precious metal and a rare wood. It was one of the most beautiful rings I'd ever seen and truly fit my betrothed's artistic personality. I opened the box, popped the top and swung around.

"You beat me to it."

His eyes immediately welled up and the tears started to flow for both of us. He was so shocked that I was going to propose to him on the same day and had found the perfect ring for the job. He removed it from the box and slipped it on. It fit, thank goodness!

We wiped tears, giggled like idiots, poured and sipped a couple of glasses of champagne while taking and posting a zillion selfies to our socials, especially of our interlocked hands now rocking each other's engagement rings. It was an incredible day. One that I had dreamed about my entire life. I could not have been happier. Or hungrier by that point!

We eventually pre-empted our engagement bliss and headed to one of his favorite Mexican restaurants in Old Town. We ate delicious food and giggled about each other's journeys to purchase the rings and our respective plans to take a knee that weekend. We walked around after lunch enjoying the sunshine, the beautiful Santa Barbara architecture, sporting our rings and the perma-smiles stretched across our faces. Sadly, by the end of the evening, I wasn't feeling so great and my betrothed was hugging the toilet barfing up everything we'd had for lunch. It was perfect. As it exactly fit how my life typically goes. Never perfectly to plan, but still utterly fantastic somehow.

He lived in Northern California so we mutually decided that I would leave my amazing job in Los Angeles and move back up to the Bay Area. It was all a bit impetuous, but the thrill of knowing that I was about to become someone's husband made it much less scary and, actually, really exciting.

I quit my job at Flipagram, packed up my stuff, bid my roommate "bye, for now" and headed up the 5 to move in with my parents. My fiancé and I struggled to figure out our living arrangements in all of the engagement hubbub as he was taking care of his elderly mother at his home, so I chose to give my parents some face time until we'd planned our next steps. I had also kept my apartment in Los Angeles because my lease was iron clad and still had another six months before it expired. Additionally, my roommate (an ex-boyfriend-turned-bestie) still needed to figure out where he was going to move. I had also designed a line of furniture being produced by the same group who had supplied the custom furniture for Flipagram. I reckoned I'd be driving down every other weekend for design and approval meetings, so it was better not to break the lease and spend alternating weekends at my fiancé's house. That way everyone was happy.

Before the move, I had scored a role as the Executive Assistant to the CEO of an augmented reality motorcycle helmet company. I had blindly reached out to the CEO via email after researching the company. I was an avid motorcyclist in Los Angeles and really wanted to work in the motorcycle industry in some capacity. The company was a media darling in the space and had become the highest-grossing campaign on IndieGoGo with over $2 million in pre-orders of their ground-breaking, augmented reality helmet. It was truly a game-changer. Beautifully designed, Bluetooth everything, and with an embedded, 180-degree, rear-view camera that projected onto a Google Glass-like, tiny screen inside the helmet that superimposed directions and information from the rear-view camera onto it. It was some Tony Stark, Ironman-level shit that was poised to make riding a motorcycle infinitesimally safer. And I was stoked to work for the guy who'd designed it.

My first day at work was telling. The company was shoehorned into an old, renovated tire change facility. It was wide open space, lined with rows of cheap, long IKEA tables, featuring a huge rollup door that let in the chilly, 40-50-degree, SF winter weather, largely unabated. Employees were full-on working in parkas and fingerless gloves and looking a little less than their chipper selves when I interviewed. I was aghast at the fact that there was no heat available anywhere within the building and, after asking, no real plans to install any. My boss, despite seemingly so well put together and collaborative during my interview cycle, quickly started showing his lack of any real managerial chops. I sensed that he was faking it a bit and needed someone like me to help get his office and staff together. But there was one of several major issues that immediately flew the red flag.

He had hired on his brother as his Chief of Staff once the company was funded. His brother was ex-military and, from the research that I had done, had not only never worked in the space, but didn't really have any relevant or conspicuous business experience of note other than working at a senior care facility in a non-management capacity. Yet, he was the type of person who had grown a little punch drunk by the money and power now at his disposal. He was the type of guy you vacillate between loving and despising, day to day. He seemed to have a really good heart but would often display behaviors and comportment that were inconsistent at best.

After only a few days in position, I was quick to conclude that some personnel changes needed to be made. One thing I always try and identify for my bosses are those on their teams who are either "hiders," in some way cancerous, or just plain incompetent. And this team was littered with all of the above. I did a bunch of impromptu interviews with several members of the team, collected info, and compiled my findings into a detailed report. I scheduled a meeting with my boss to go over my thoughts. He asked me to accompany him to dinner that evening at "The Battery," a private club for young entrepreneurs and the nouveau riche, business elite of San Francisco.

We hopped in his recently purchased Audi R8 supercar and headed for the club. I'm a car guy, especially German cars, so I began reciting stats and figures about the car much to his shock and delight. In an effort to impress me, he took a right turn just a bit too hard on the gas on the notoriously fog-slickened, train-tracked San Francisco streets and fishtailed for about 200 yards as he struggled to regain control of the car. And his pride. He looked over at me to gauge whether or not I was shitting my pants or white knuckling the dashboard. I wasn't. Velocity and I have been friends since I was a young child when my father would often do the same thing in his souped-up, Now-and-later colored, Datsun 240Z. I, in turn, looked over at him to make sure he wasn't white knuckling the steering wheel and suggested he loosen his grip next time and let the car sort itself out with minimal input and a lighter touch on the throttle. The entire time I'm thinking, "Somebody needs to learn how to drive their shit," and further confirming that rich people are just as inept as all of us.

We chatted openly in the car about my findings and eventually made it to The Battery. We ordered drinks and dinner and continued the discussion. I suggested that several people should be relieved of their duties or reassigned. One included the person who had held the role before I joined the company. She was a young woman who was nice enough, but whom I could tell had grown jaded and bitter in position and was displaying the tell-tale "I don't give a fuck" attitude toward her responsibilities, especially toward my boss and his brother. Little did I know she would be a treasure trove of information about the two co-founders' shady financial practices that would eventually get them booted from their own company and embroiled in a nasty, wrongful termination lawsuit with the same young woman.

In total, I suggested that six employees be cut from the team and apparently it hadn't fallen on deaf ears. Within two days several people were given notice of their dismissal, including the ex-

Assistant. The timing couldn't have been worse as it was only 2 days before the company holiday party. Of course, as the new Assistant, I was on the hook to save the event which had become a hybrid effort with two other, high profile organizations in the tech scene whose guests we were also hosting at our facility. I got as much information as I could from the outgoing Assistant, but it was clear I was on my own.

Since many of the vendors had been chosen by the previous Assistant, most of whom were friends of hers, my voicemail and email quickly filled with cancellations. The band quit. Then the caterer quit. Then the DJ quit. Complete fucking nightmare. Of course, I told my boss that his timing couldn't have been worse but assured him it wasn't my first rodeo and I'd work it all out. I still had a pretty full Rolodex of vendors I'd worked with from my Silicon Valley event planning days. I had also performed and remained friends with a number of incredible musicians I'd performed with locally and around the world in numerous bands. I started making phone calls and was able to quickly confirm a new band and hire a caterer who could fulfil the last-minute request. Luckily, one of the sponsors of the event was responsible for the alcohol which is always the easiest solve anytime shit goes pear-shaped. Liquor 'em up and they'll quickly forgive. And, indeed, they did!

It was a scramble, but the event came together and went off without a hitch. The band was insane, comprised of individual musicians who had performed with Stevie Wonder, Lauren Hill, Aretha Franklin, even Whitesnake. All of the party guests showed up and had an incredible time. In fact, there were about 50 people still partying away at 1:30 am on a Thursday night, long after the party had officially ended. People were quick to sing my praises to my new boss who was visibly proud of the fact that he had scored the ex-Assistant to the President of Levi's and Jack Dorsey in his corner and was actually doing everything I said I would do, and then some. The rest of the team quickly noted that I was a force to be reckoned with and had either grown suspicious of me or become excited that they finally had a resource to go to that wasn't either of the brothers. The party was one thing, but I knew I needed a much more conspicuous win in order for the team to truly trust me.

I'd insisted on fixing the heat issue as it was often unbearable to work in the building on chilly days. Quickly budget was allocated to get the electrical wiring updated and industrial, overhead heat lamps were installed in the rafters. Done. To my horror, our pay cycles were monthly vs. bi-weekly like 99% of businesses in the history of ever. My boss was clueless about how imperative it was to change this and signed off on it immediately. Done. My stock with the team quickly increased, exponentially. More importantly, the team felt that they now had an ally in me, and I witnessed the once, severely flagging morale begin to take a turn toward the positive. We still had issues, especially with the co-founders, but things were definitely better than when I'd first walked through the door.

We were in the process of redesigning the company's website and my boss made me a project manager. My role was to preview any changes to the site and make sure they were all executed to my and his standards prior to him reviewing them. The gentleman spearheading the website redesign was one of the people I had actually suggested being relieved of duty. He often worked in a silo and made it virtually impossible to meet with him to discuss ideas and changes. Additionally, he worked at snail's pace to the point where it was painful to get from rev to rev with any sense of urgency. I'd surmised that he wasn't really that good anyway and could be replaced overnight with a phone call or two to my vast network of web design friends from previous companies.

This all came to a head on New Year's Day. I had flown to Seattle with my fiancé to celebrate New Year's and meet several of his friends excited to meet the man their friend had proposed to. We had a freezing, but incredible New Year's Eve. I woke on New Year's Day to the sound of my phone buzzing uncontrollably. My boss had called and emailed incessantly with numerous "911" messages. I called and he launched into a tirade that the website was down and that I needed to take care of it ASAP. Of course, I sprang into action. I immediately called the Marketing Director and he never picked up nor returned even one of my calls. I emailed him as well. Nothing. It was inexcusable, especially knowing that the new site was going live on New Year's Eve. There was no contingency plan in place and the site was intermittently down or barely functional for many hours. I ended up canceling lunch and dinner with my fiancé's friends to try and rectify the website issue, which caused a nasty argument with my fiancé. He barely spoke to me for the remaining two days of the trip and I eventually reminded him that he knew what he had signed up for when proposing to me, fully knowing that the nature of my job precluded I be available 24/7/365. Little did I know it would signify rough waters ahead.

My fiancé, and I too, had grown increasingly frustrated with the constant phone calls and texts from my boss. He would contact me at all hours of the day and night often with strange requests for freshly-squeezed green juice at, like, 3 am in the morning. I'd assume he was drunk from the night before and let him know that I would have juice messengered to his house once the juice shop was actually open for business. His behavior seemed a bit erratic and excessive, but I waved it off as him being a clueless, new CEO stoked with my ability to create magic, but unfamiliar with the actual protocol and level of service I was providing him. My fiancé found the entire relationship with my boss ridiculous and invasive and quickly grew frustrated with me for what he'd perceived as enabling inexcusable behavior.

The Consumer Electronics Show (CES) in Las Vegas was looming. Much to my chagrin, I found out that we had not registered for a booth but would still be attending and meeting with several potential investors interested in joining our impending Series C fundraising round. We were hurrying to build a number of prototype helmets in order to "gonzo" the event by simply walking around the trade show floor offering impromptu demonstrations of the helmet. "Gonzo" meaning our Marketing Director had dropped the ball on securing a space at the tradeshow to debut the helmet properly. Additionally, I had scheduled 2 full days of meetings with potential investors to meet my boss and receive detailed demos of the helmets. I volunteered to rent a big-ass SUV and drive the helmets to the show myself. I wanted to eradicate any possibility of damage or theft of the helmets, especially given they were shipping to Las Vegas during one of the biggest, craziest conferences of the calendar year and one of the most sought-after products on the planet that had yet to hit the market. We rushed to prepare the prototypes, loaded them into the SUV, and I made the 8-hour drive to Las Vegas from San Francisco.

Las Vegas during CES was an exercise in frustration for me. The roads were a joke. Traffic was a level of insane that even I wasn't prepared for having lived in LA for a couple of years prior. And parking success was often dependent on the closeness of your relationship with God.

I managed to do my best as chauffeur for my boss and the scant support crew who came along to CES and walk the floor with the helmets offering impromptu demos. One instance, in particular, threw me a bit for a loop. I had just dropped off my boss and another co-worker at the entrance to the main hall at CES after over 30 minutes of driving in circles looking for parking. I eventually found a hotel nearby that would allow me to valet for the low, low price of $50. My boss was uncharacteristically agitated for some reason and was annoying the shit of out of me in return, so it was a nice respite to be without him for the 30 minutes it took to find parking. I met up with him on the trade show floor which was teaming with conference attendees and merchants. It was extremely crowded, loud, and frenetic. A couple of hours in I noticed my boss was sweating profusely and constantly asking me for water. He didn't seem quite right, so I kept a bit more of a paternal eye on him while shuttling him from booth-to-booth and meeting-to-meeting with journalists and potential investors. Nothing was running on time as you can imagine with all of the insanity on the trade show floor and with traffic outside being such a shit show. After another hour, my boss pulled my arm, spun me around and screamed, "Get me outta here! Now!" I could see in his eyes the tell-tale sign that he was having an anxiety attack. I had a feeling something was up with his behavior from earlier in the day, and this validated it.

I grabbed him by the shoulder and started beating a path to where I thought the exits might be. It was almost impossible to find the exits on the trade show floor from the center of the action because all of the towering displays blocked any sort of conspicuous exit sign designating an escape route. It quickly became a practice of walking several yards and asking where the exits were. Walking in the direction they pointed for a few more yards, asking again, and repeating the process. It took us almost 10 minutes to eventually find the exits. By the time we found them my boss had lost color in his face. I immediately rushed him downstairs, out of the convention center, and onto the street for some fresh air. I called one of the team members inside to come and stay with him while I beat a path to the SUV. As you can imagine it was a nightmare just trying to navigate the bumper-to-bumper traffic jam back to where they were waiting. My boss called me numerous times while I was stuck in traffic and I suggested they walk in my direction and meet me and at least get out of the heat.

"Uh, yeah, that's not gonna happen."

After almost 20 minutes I finally got to where I'd expected to meet them. There were no familiar faces in sight. So, I called my co-worker since I was a snap away from cursing out my boss for the previous fucked up comment.

"Hey, where are you guys? I'm right in front of the pickup point."

"He had to pee so we started walking up the street so that he could duck into one of the casinos to use the restroom."

I was FURIOUS. Not only had they walked in the opposite direction of where I was, it was going to take me a minimum of 30 minutes to get to a place where I could turn around to try and pick them up. And, of course, my boss was blowing up my phone with calls and texts asking where I was. It was the most frustrating experience I've ever had and has made me loathe the whole Las Vegas conference experience to this day.

We finally met up at the next meeting spot and managed to hobble through the rest of the day exchanging few pleasantries and lots of silence. Once the final meeting of the day had concluded I dropped off the crew and headed to my hotel room to recharge the helmets, grab dinner, and pass out from being emotionally and physically spent. At 4 am the next morning I received a text message from my boss requesting a beard trimmer and a cup of coffee. As you can imagine I was instantly annoyed. And then I thought, "Wait, he doesn't even have a beard!" Given that he was a gorgeous, vain man I could only surmise that there was about to be some manscaping going on, because he certainly wasn't about to use that thing on his perfectly coiffed head of beautiful hair. I couldn't help but be annoyed that he'd ask at 4 am in the fucking morning, fully expecting me to crush the request like I always did. And, of course, I did.

I quickly dressed, did a Google search for open drug stores, jumped in the SUV and headed to a 24-hour CVS several miles away. I purchased his stupid beard trimmer, picked up a large coffee from the only coffee option available at 4:30 am, a Jack in the Box drive-thru, parked the SUV and knocked on his door to deliver the goods with just enough resting bitch face to telegraph my disapproval of the off-hours request.

He thanked me profusely. I reminded him of his schedule for the day and that checkout was at noon and beat a path back to my hotel room to get ready for the day. I packed up everything, loaded up the SUV and waited for his arrival several hours later to begin our final day of meetings. One of the vendors who'd helped manufacture the helmet had graciously offered up a portion of their rather glamorous presentation space to display our helmet and run live demos. It worked out perfectly as we were able to display the helmet alongside many game-changing products the company had produced and held numerous meetings and demos with potential investors both within the venue and on the couches scattered just outside of the presentation rooms. The meetings went well and landed several promises of investment in the round.

"Hey, I noticed you didn't bring any bags down. Did you check out of your hotel room?"

"Shit. No, I forgot. Can you just arrange a late checkout for me with the hotel? I'll go back and pack up later."

"No. I already checked on availability and they are booked solid because there's a conference immediately after CES. Just give me your room key. I'll go pack you up right now."

I noticed he was a bit hesitant but handed me his key and apologized for me having to navigate the mess he'd left. I drove back to the hotel and entered his room. Let's just say that I now tip hotel cleaning staff obscenely because having to deal with the state that room was in was definitely deserving of enough money to either get a massage or have a nice dinner having to do that shit on a daily basis. There were clothes strewn everywhere. I started pulling clothes off of lampshades, the floor, and trying to discern and segregate clean from dirty while folding and packing frantically as it was quickly closing in on checkout time. I walked into the bathroom and was mortified that he had thrown the discarded box of his beard trimmer in the bathtub along with any and all cardboard and trash that he'd accumulated throughout his visit. I had located and purchased him tons of fresh juice from a juice shop several miles out of town and found all of the discarded bottles in the bathtub. Oh! and I'd confirmed that the beard trimmer was definitely not for his beard as evidenced by the clippings I found on the bathroom floor that looked suspiciously wirier and curlier than the hair on his head. #winning

There was a humungous, Ziplock bag filled with prescription medication bottles. While I was curious to see where his mania was emanating from, I was more interested in knocking out the packing and getting back to managing the numerous investor meetings at the venue. I managed to get everything packed up quickly, returned the keys to the front desk, and headed back to the venue.

The rest of the day went to plan. We had several meetings with big investors including one who had just invested in Fitbit. I ended up running into HGTV royalty, The Property Brothers, who were preparing for a live presentation. They were very tall, incredibly handsome, and super gracious in accommodating my request for a quick photo.

We ended up wrapping at the event around 6 pm that evening. I was going to drive the SUV back to my apartment in LA, spend the weekend there and hang with my roommate, head back to San Francisco to drop off the helmets at the office and return the SUV. I dropped the group off at the airport and I remember my boss pulling something from the bag I'd packed, quickly jamming something else inside the bag, then asking that I take the bag home with me and bring it to the office when I got back. I suggested it would be quicker for him to take it on the plane, but he insisted he didn't need it and to just leave it in his office once I got back to San Francisco. In all honesty, I was over him after a week of CES stress, so I agreed, bid them all farewell, and got on the road to Los Angeles.

I got to my apartment, hung out with my roommate for a bit and decompressed for a day and a half in sunny Los Angeles. I drove back to San Francisco that Sunday, dropped off the helmets, his bag, and returned the SUV to the airport.

One morning about a week later, while at work, I received a call from my mother informing me that my grandmother had passed away. She had found her non-responsive upon entering her apartment that morning. It was jarring news and a bit difficult to process given all I'd just gone through. My mom knew all that I was dealing with at work and insisted that I continue doing what I was doing. I let my boss know the news and he insisted that I take care of myself and my mother as needed.

We quickly planned the memorial service and I remember on the day of it receiving a series of texts from my boss saying, "I know you're busy, but…" or "When you come up for air, can you…" I don't know what possessed me to keep my phone on during my grandmother's memorial service, but the fact that someone had the fucking nerve to text their grieving employee with non-urgent, to-do list items was unfathomable to me. I knew then my days at the company were numbered.

The brothers decided to buy a dog who would quickly become the company mascot. It was a super cute, black and white, Pitbull puppy that was growing in inquisitiveness almost as quickly as it grew in size. The dog was already pretty wild when I met it and was already enrolled in obedience training. Unfortunately, neither my boss nor his brother attended the classes with much regularity, so the dog would resume its wild, inquisitive, disobedience much to the chagrin of my co-workers who would either witness items left under their desks being chewed through or suddenly smelling the numerous little presents the dog would leave under random desks throughout the day. I absolutely refused to add dog watcher and poop scooper to my job description and made that expressly clear to both my boss and his brother. I'd ended a relationship because of a dog once so I wanted nothing to do with the distraction, especially at a professional level.

One day, the brother showed up with the puppy rocking what I quickly surmised to be a shock collar. He had a remote that he placed on his desk as if proudly finding the solution to world hunger. I was disgusted and vehemently verbalized my displeasure. The one thing that never sits well with me is anyone feeling that they have the right to inflict pain on another living being.

The puppy liked to bark. It was a puppy, for fuck's sake. We had created a biergarten in the courtyard that led to the front entrance and there were often birds that would land on tables or on the fence. The dog, like dogs do, would bark and chase them as far as his leash would allow. And now, armed with his new torture device, the brother would blithely pick up the remote, hit a button, and we would quickly hear a pained yelp from the dog and silence thereafter. The first time I witnessed it my eyes welled up. It was clear torture to me, and it sickened me to my core. It happened numerous times that day and I snapped. I told the brother to knock it off or I was leaving. He found my outrage amusing but agreed to go easy on the button. While he was away from his desk, I snagged the remote and hid it in my desk drawer. This whole bullshit adventure had to end.

One morning I was working away. The brother came into the office with the puppy. Had gotten him all set up outside and walked over to his desk to sit down. He reached behind him pulled out this large, 8" bowie knife and loudly stabbed it into the top of his butcher block desk. Now, I don't know about you, but that seemed not only crazy, but a big-ass, tasty lawsuit opportunity handed to anyone in the building who'd witnessed such ridiculousness. I'm pretty hard to rattle so I went in on him.

"What the hell? Dude take that knife out of the desk. There are women in this building, and you look hella crazy right now."

He thought it was hilarious and refused to extract the knife. I reminded him that there were women in the building and that his actions could be litigious to the company. His brother's company.

"No one's gonna sue us."

Famous last words.

There was an employee who worked at the company whom I just couldn't figure out. He was sometimes an errand boy. He would often be dispatched to go and retrieve my boss' car from The Battery numerous times per week, which I found odd. He also did some handiwork around the building, so I assumed he was a general-purpose Assistant. However, I'd often find him at his desk in the remotest corner of the building snoring away. I asked my boss about him and he mentioned that he was hired to be a bodyguard during the product tour for the helmet. He was hired on afterward because he was a bit of a hard luck case and was taking care of his family with his salary. I suggested that I become his supervisor so that I could give him meatier projects to work on and also manage his workload. The snoring thing would normally get you fired but was a tell-tale sign of underutilization. He agreed and allowed me to make the reporting change.

I spent quite a bit of time talking to my new charge. He was an intelligent guy and had an interesting story. He was super helpful, but I could also tell he wasn't all that interested in climbing any kind of corporate ladder. He was cool chilling in the shadows and would often disappear for hours to handle external requests for my boss that they had brokered without my knowledge.

One afternoon my boss had pissed me off royally. His constant waffling and inconsistent behavior were really starting to take a toll on me. I was used to working for billionaires who knew how to utilize and treat an Assistant of my pedigree. This kid had no fucking clue. My name had magically morphed to "Jeeves" and he had me running in more circles than a track star. In combination with his crazy ass brother I was pretty much at my wit's end. I grabbed a soda from the fridge and went to sit outside in the biergarten by myself to try and decompress. My new charge came outside randomly and could tell that I wasn't happy.

"Let me guess."

"Yep. He's fucking out of control today. I'm so over it."

"Yeah, he's on one alright."

"Why, is he bugging you too much? Let me know and I'll talk to him."

"No, he's on one. Probably from last night still."

I looked at him completely confused.

"Wait. You know why I'm here, right?"

Again, my best confused face.

"I'm his supplier. I bring him drugs almost every night."

Holy. Fucking. Shit. It all made sense. Instantaneously. All of the random 2 and 3 am phone calls and texts asking for fresh juice and immunity boosters. The senselessly erratic behavior. The BBC interview I had brokered that he showed up late to, puffy and sweating, and speaking way too loudly. His mood swings. His short fuse. I even thought about the bag incident in Vegas which just didn't make sense. It was a foil to get me to take a bag of something in the SUV with me that wouldn't clear TSA. The calls during my grandmother's memorial service. The fight he caused on New Year's Day with my fiancé. It all made sense and it made me sick to my stomach.

My charge went on to tell me stories of the wild, drugged fueled nights they had across the world on the helmet tour. One particular incident in Miami was regaled. My boss, an Assistant and he had hung out after a press event. They decided to paint the town which included my charge scoring some drugs for my boss. They partied for a while and my charge decided to call it a night, reminding my boss to go easy on the drugs and partying as they had a flight to catch the following morning. And with that he returned to his hotel room.

"One of my buddies called me around 1 am telling me that they'd had to apprehend my boss and put him in an ambulance. He said it was the funniest thing they'd ever seen."

My boss was allegedly being belligerent and combative but appeared to be fast asleep, but vertical. He was throwing punches, but he was literally sleeping standing up. They finally wrestled him to the ground, still sleeping but punching, and called for an ambulance. My boss, allegedly, spent several hours in the ER getting his stomach pumped to remove all of the drugs he'd ingested. According to my charge, pretty much everything he'd scored for him had made it into my boss' body. Which should have killed him. Luckily, his bouncer friends who fended off the sleeping boxer had the foresight to call an ambulance which likely saved his life.

So here I am listening away to story after story wondering how the hell I got here. Supporting someone fighting with drug addiction. His brother torturing dogs and stabbing knives into desks. Spending company money on personal shit like juice and gifts and apartments and cars and motorcycles. I had warned the CFO numerous times that the brothers were guilty of conversion and that he had better do something about it before all hell broke loose with the investors. The CFO was about as effective as a hairbrush during a typhoon. He agreed that something had to be done but felt too neutered to do anything.

That day, my boss and I were finishing up the final email package that would be sent out to all of the potential Series C investors we'd met with at CES in Vegas. It was originally being pulled together by the incompetent Marketing dude who fucked up my New Years with his absence. I took it over as I'd worked on similar emails during my time working at investment banks and VCs. I knew how the content should be presented and I helped to write the copy.

My boss, his brother and their girlfriends decided to celebrate by heading to Napa for the weekend. I found and booked them accommodations. We settled on the verbiage for the investor email and all of the attachments. My boss and brothers left and began their drive to Napa. I began emailing the information to all of the investors on the list. I quickly got a phone call asking me to stop what I was doing.

"Dude, the font color is showing up purple on the email. It looks like you're copying and pasting!"

For some reason, sending via Google Mail converted copied and pasted text into this random purple color. Despite my best efforts to mitigate it and turning each subsequent copy/paste to black text, upon sending it would turn back to purple. I bcc'd my boss on all of the emails I sent. Some went off with black text. Some still converted the text to purple. And he became more and more agitated.

The night had already grown long. I had showed up at 7:30 am that morning. Heard from my charge that I was supporting someone who was allegedly drug addicted. And now dealing with someone essentially calling me incompetent and low-key blaming me for potentially ruining deals because the investors would be receiving purple text signifying, they're in some way not "special."

"Dude, this is exhausting. I really need to know if you're in this or not."

Ladies and gentlemen: THE LAST STRAW.

"You know what? Let's just call it. It's not working so let's call it for what it is."

I think he was truly taken aback by my response. But at that point I really didn't care.

"I'm really sorry to hear that. But I understand."

And just like that, I'd quit. And I never felt a bigger rush of relief in my life since.

I closed down my laptop, grabbed a few of my personal effects and bounced. I emailed the CFO to let him know what had just transpired and that I would meet him first thing in the morning to return my keys, corporate credit card and sign anything he needed me to sign.

I showed up the next morning, walked upstairs, handed him all of the company-issued items and had a brief exit interview.

"So, you're leaving us, huh?"

"Yep!"

"Too much work?"

"Nope. The workload was fine. I just don't like the man. And it's kind of important for me to like the person I support. He's a nice guy and all, but I just don't like him."

We exchanged a few more pleasantries, I peaced-out my favorite two employees and left the building for the final time. I got to my car and immediately hopped on Facebook.

"If anyone is looking for a kick-ass Executive Assistant, please let me know. I'm available!"

And with that, I headed back home.

Several hours later I received a call from my fiancé who'd read my Facebook post and wanted to chat about it. I told him that I was wiped out and that I was going to take a nap and call him a bit later. I could tell he was a little upset, but we agreed to chat the following morning. I crashed for several hours, exhausted from all of the emotion from just that month alone, and spent numerous hours on LinkedIn looking for my next role and contacting my recruiter of 15 years to rally her help.

The next morning my fiancé called. He was upset with me for finding out via social media that I had quit my job. I was originally going to call him at work that day but knew that he was super busy and didn't want my situation to be a distraction. Plus, given all of the turmoil of my grandmother's death, all of the ruined or interrupted plans at the hands of my ex-boss, and living apart and seeing each other only every other weekend, I was a little threadbare.

He lectured me on communication, and I apologized for the perceived disrespect. I live on social media and I needed to get the word out in case someone knew of an opening that I could swoop in on. But I understood where he was coming from. Then he hit me with it.

"I'm so sorry, but I don't think I can do this anymore. It's just too much for me right now."

Silence.

He went on to explain that my work dramas were taking their toll. Also, the fact that I spent so much time away from him was manifesting in him missing me and not feeling that I was as committed as he was. And the stress of also having to take care of his ailing and aging mother had just become too much to deal with and had, clearly, overcomplicated his life.

"Why don't we revisit this in, like, six months?"

Ladies and gentlemen: RAGE.

"Revisit what in six months? Us? Are you fucking kidding me right now?"

I reminded him that I'd quit my perfect job at Flipagram to move up North to be at least near him since we hadn't worked out our living situation. I also reminded him that he had asked me to marry him which means through better or worse and that it was a forever agreement. If he didn't feel "forever" now, he likely wouldn't in six months either.

He quickly grew wary of the conversation and suggested we speak later. I told him that wasn't necessary and quickly got off the phone.

I was devastated. Like, to the very core of my being in the space of a phone conversation. And it was compounding as every second ticked away. In a rage I got up, grabbed every empty piece of luggage I had and began stuffing it full of my clothes. My mom swung by my room to see what all the ruckus was, and I let her know that my fiancé had broken off our engagement and I was going back to Los Angeles. NOW. She tried her best to calm me down but knew that, like her, once I make up my mind to do something, I can't be deterred. I quickly packed my little Fiat with all of my possessions, hugged and kissed my parents and headed for I-5.

I played every sad song I knew and cried audibly for the majority of the 5-hour drive back to LA. Thank God I had the foresight not to try and break that lease. It quickly became my refuge for the next three weeks. Just like that scene from the Sex and City movie after Carrie had been left at the alter by Big and the girls joined her in

Mexico on what was supposed to be her honeymoon. I too, drew the blinds, locked my door and disappeared into an abyss of sadness so deep and so painful I barely had energy breathe. It felt like everything had fallen apart in the space of six weeks. I'd quit my dream job. I'd gotten engaged to and cast off by one of my best friends and loves of my life. I'd lost the woman who'd raised me. I had gotten duped by a CEO I had such high hopes for with a product that could change the world and save scores of lives. And now I was back in LA, weeping uncontrollably, alone, and left to pick up the pieces. Pretty fucked up, if you ask me.

My roommate was there to pick up the pieces as best he could. We were exes so he knew when to just leave me in silence and when to pop his head in to make sure I wasn't hanging from the ceiling fan. I communicated a couple of times with my ex-fiancé', ironically over social media, and insisted that he give me space. I was hurt, disappointed and angry and now dealing with having no income, so the very last person I wanted to talk to was him. He quickly became the blame for all of this, so I implored of him to just disappear. He did, for the most part. A few of his apologetic emails were met with eye rolls and non-replies. And, eventually, he ceased contact.

The balance of the year was one of the most surreal, horrible times of my life. I ended up receiving a call from the CEO of the company that was producing my furniture line. He was looking for a replacement COO for a new, luxury home staging business he had purchased and thought that I would be a great fit. His current COO was moving up North and was vacating the spot. We met up and chatted about the opportunity and I decided to give it a go. Mostly out of desperation, but definitely out of curiosity. What better way to right the ship than to join the C-suite...as a C-suiter?

My first day on the job was a meeting with the team at their manufacturing facility in South Central LA. It was their regular Monday morning status where they talked about work in the queue as well as upcoming jobs. After the meeting I sat with the outgoing COO.

"Can you show me the books?"

He was a bit reluctant but showed me numerous spreadsheets that detailed the financials and the budget numbers for the arm of the business that

I would be assuming as COO. I stared at the numbers quizzically and asked a few clarifying questions. You know how you squint at something sometimes that's so unbelievable expecting it to magically morph and make sense? Well, those numbers didn't. At all.

I was pretty proud of myself for recognizing, in the moment, that the numbers were a mess. All those years as an Executive Assistant looking at balance sheets and budgeting the $70 million in financing at Flipagram as their interim Controller gave me the ability to run the numbers in my head, and based on their projections, I recognized a revenue shortfall that would barely allow them to make their upcoming payroll cycle, let alone pay me. What the whole fuck?

I quickly excused myself, claiming that I wanted to head back home and sit with the numbers for a bit. The moment I got home I wrote my resignation letter to the CEO expressing my horror at what I'd seen. Given all I was going through it was beginning to feel like the Universe was conspiring against me.

Lessons Learned

Never ignore a red flag.

One thing I teach is to always pay attention to red flags, especially in the interviewing process. Inevitably one or two will pop up in conversation with the slightly-too-eager HR rep or the time-constrained Executive whom you can sense is not really present, constantly checking his cell, or having distracted eyeballs while you're looking him straight in his. I always say to take any red flag that pops up, multiply them by three, and that's what you can expect on a day-to-day basis. In other words, those are confirmation of the real person and behavior you'll get once you sign on the dotted line. It is, easily, the most accurate and sound advice I give and is applicable in all parts of your life, not just business.

Trust your instincts. They're always right.

My initial red flags with this particular CEO was that he was in a field that was in no way related to his area of expertise. And during the interview, I remembered feeling that he was a bit too buttoned up and coming across as a bit of an imposter. He was wearing glasses, but I noticed no tell-tale magnification in the lenses and hadn't noticed him sporting glasses in any of his photos all over Internet. Fake. He was asking what he considered to be probing questions, but none ever made it out of third gear, especially when I'd already worked from two game-changing CEOs. No one in the building looked happy. There was no spontaneous burst of laughter, fist bumps, bro hugs, nothing. Only my handlers were dispensing the smiles and even those seemed measured. All of these things would later confirm my 3x theory. Working at that company was not fun. The CEO was not ready. In fact, he was a hot fucking mess. And, eventually, I ended up leaving the company because I'd looked past the red flags for a sweet salary, a cool product, an opportunity to be near my betrothed. Notice, it all went up in flames in a matter of months.

Your shitty job is a choice you make. And that choice affects more than just you.

Walter had every right to call things off. The insanity that the CEO exacted on my life affected my personal relationship greatly. In retrospect, I realize that we talked more about my boss' shenanigans than we did about our wedding plans. Dinners were interrupted by drug-fueled requests from my boss. Early mornings that used to be dominated by cuddle time, were preempted by me constantly reaching for my phone. Canceling dinner with his best friends who were excited to meet me was, I'm sure, one of the final straws that ended our relationship. And as much as I blamed Walter for months for our broken engagement and my destroyed heart, I came to realize that I couldn't exonerate myself from the decision.

STORY #8: WEVR

Within a week I ended up getting a random contact request from a recruiter who had seen my resume on LinkedIn. He had on Operations role at a virtual reality startup in Venice and thought I could be a great fit. We quickly scheduled an interview and within days I was deep into the interviewing process.

I met with both co-founders of the company and really liked them both. However, they had polar opposite personalities. The CEO was very sweet, soft-spoken, pensive, and struck me as potentially being a little passive-aggressive. Noted. The Head of Design was my type of guy. Brash. To the point. Design-led. And gave me the vibe of an ex-skateboarder bro turned design god. I liked elements of both of their personalities, but I could tell something was amiss. Upon having lunch with both of them, separately, I discovered that they gave me completely different visions for the company. Like, not even close. And, as we approached the offer phase, I told them as much. It was my one red flag that I needed one or both of them to clear up for me. The CEO was adamant that they were aligned and that I may have mistaken the other's passion. I hadn't. And I needed a job. They offered the largest salary I'd ever had at the time and I took it.

The company was a mess. Employee morale was extremely low. There were a number of cancerous employees who I'd identified within the first week of my employ. I had many impromptu conversations with the employees and quickly ascertained that none of them had trust in the leadership abilities of the CEO nor the co-founder. I quickly found out why.

My CEO ended up throwing me squarely under the bus within a month of being in position. We had an intern who had just left the company to return to his native country. He was an awesome kid and beloved by everyone. My boss and I were in New York City to attend investor meetings and do a number of demos or our VR experiences around the city. While there, our intern had broadcast a beautifully crafted goodbye email from his personal blog accidentally revealing a top-secret project that he had worked on which hadn't yet been released to the public. He didn't have a large online following and, in retrospect, didn't pose much of a threat, but the fact that a company secret was being distributed by an ex-employee triggered a swift reaction. My boss texted me and asked if I'd seen the email. I confirmed that I had. He asked that I reach out to the manager of the ex-intern and ask him to take that portion out of his blog as it was in breach of our company's non-disclosure agreement, which he had signed as terms of his employment. I did, without much fanfare, and the manager did as asked. The ex-intern felt terrible and rewrote the blog entry ASAP. My boss, however, wasn't satisfied and wanted to send a message to the company about the severity of the breach. Since I had sent many of those low-key threatening emails while working for the General Counsel at Square as well as during my time at Levi Strauss, I quickly drafted a similar email and sent it off to my boss to approve. He read it, approved it, but asked that I send it from my email address. I found that odd since it was an important email about a security breach and should likely come from him, the CEO. However, I agreed, addressed it accordingly and shot it off.

I woke up the next morning to an absolute firestorm. Managers roasted me via email and were angry and offended by the perceived terseness of the email. They'd assumed that I had overstepped my authority and were demanding a public apology to the entire team. My boss called me in a panic and asked what to do. I told him, I'd send a follow-up email apologizing for the perceived disrespect and terse language. He agreed and said that he would then follow-up with an email backing me up and explaining that no harm was intended.

I crafted an exculpatory email stating that I'd worked in Legal departments at two multi-billion-dollar corporations and the email I sent was a rather normal reaction to any security breach I'd encountered at either of those companies. While that particular breach of company information was still a serious issue, I could have been a bit more selective with my words. "Sorry 'bout that." Sent.

Within 15 minutes, my boss sent his follow-up email. But instead of backing me up as originally promised he publicly admonished me for sending the original email and stated that "we need be more careful and thoughtful with our words" as to not create unnecessary divisions and misunderstandings within the group.

What. The Whole. FUCK?!

I was furious. This year was turning out to be a complete fucking joke. I was losing all respect for anyone with a C-level title because they were all, clearly, fucked in the head.

I ended up getting thrown under the bus numerous more times by that CEO and finally decided I'd had enough. Ironically, the same CEO from the company I'd quit after only three hours reached out to me and offered me a new COO role and percentage partnership in the new business. He'd poached the top salesperson from of our chief competitor in the luxury home staging space who had already booked millions of dollars of new business for the new company. He needed me to immediately come and gain control of operations, promising the company was more than solvent and tracking to quickly become one of the top luxury staging companies on the scene. In yet another act of desperation, I agreed and submitted my two weeks' notice at the VR company.

One day I ran into the other co-founder while he was parking his car. He had become a little cold toward me, but we managed to strike up a quick conversation. He could tell I was a little threadbare and asked what was up. I told him that I felt I was frustrated because I was constantly being thrown under the bus by the CEO. I told him about the terse email incident while I was in NYC with my boss and he started laughing loudly and shaking his head.

"You got Nevilled, my friend."

He went on to explain that this was a consistent pattern of passive-aggressive behavior by my boss that warranted its own adjective. He was actually relieved to hear that I hadn't acted as a lone wolf and that his co-founder was the one who had actually requested, I send that email. He had pretty much written me off as out of control and a minion of my boss and had warned the other members of his team to avoid any unnecessary contact with me at all costs. He apologized profusely at the misperception, gave me a big hug and welcomed me to the club as an official member of "The Nevilled." Lovely.

My final duty in position was a doozy. The cooler of the two co-founders had been invited by Unilever to give a keynote speech at their annual conference and run VR demos for select members of their leadership team. The co-founder had agreed to doing the keynote months prior. About a week before the event he chose not to go and insisted another member of the team present in his place. This caused a firestorm of epic proportions throughout the events team at Unilever who had passed on several bonafide celebrities as their keynote speaker in favor of the VR darling that the co-founder had become. I did my best to calm everyone down and we decided to send the co-founder's next-in-command. The issue was this employee, though freakin' brilliant, was he had a thick and often difficult to understand accent. The Unilever events team was aware of who he was after a few quick YouTube searches and expressed concern that he may be too hard to understand and didn't possess the same character and presence as the co-founder. I assured them that he was more than capable of delivering the goods and I'd make sure he blew their socks off. I also decided to attend the show and single-handedly setup the equipment and run the demos, something I had never done alone before. However, one of my employees who normally handled these responsibilities needed to remain behind to run demos for an important series of meetings while I was away.

I quickly learned the nuances of setting up the equipment and took tons of iPhone videos to document the play-by-play of setting up the machinery. I packed everything up and off I went. I met up with the events crew and they thanked me for pulling everything together and for calming their panic. I, of course, didn't tell them that I had already given notice of my departure and that I was there as more of a courtesy than an obligation. I quickly set up the equipment and got it running, hitch-free. I grabbed lunch with the employee giving the keynote and had an amazing conversation with him as well. We managed to dispel the same misperception of me that his boss had and he, too, laughed at my being "Nevilled."

I waited a floor below where the keynote was taking place and soon a steady stream of people began filling the area asking for a demo. I started putting VR goggles on each of them, one after another, and running them through our insanely popular VR experiences to amazed faces and an endless stream of oohs and ahs. Suddenly, the throng parted, and three gentlemen appeared along with several TV cameras. Another employee abruptly ended the current VR session with a tap on the shoulder and removing the goggles. Apparently, I was in the presence of the CEO of Unilever and two of his top team members. He mentioned that he had never done VR before but was excited to give it a try. I assured him that it was going to blow his mind and proceeded to affix the goggles to his head. I started the experience and watched him get lost in the seascape and react to the various sea life designed into the experience.

"Look left."

I knew that the money shot was about to happen. A huge, insanely realistic whale would be swimming by at that moment appearing, in VR, less than three feet away within the experience. He suddenly jumped backward.

"Holy shit!"

Everyone in the room burst into laughter. He smiled and reached out his hands holding the controllers and was amazed that things reacted to his gestures. It was a slam dunk. He removed the goggles when the experience ended and thanked me profusely. He said it was the most incredible experience he'd ever had that far exceeded his expectations.

One of his partners came over to me to thank me for pulling everything together. He'd heard of the dramas from his team but was told that I was incredibly helpful, professional, and an absolute joy to work with. He mentioned that he'd be in touch shortly to book a follow-up meeting with my CEO to further ascertain how to partner with Unilever. Not a bad way to go out, eh?

Upon returning to work, word had gotten to my boss and the co-founder that the event was a smashing success. My boss, of course, said nothing. The cooler co-founder made a special trip to my building to thank me for saving our participation in the event.

"I won't lie, I thought you were just going to phone it in. You'd already quit so I didn't have high hopes. But you killed it. I got, like, four emails praising you and telling me the event was an overwhelming success. So, thank you. Seriously."

"C'mon now! You know I wouldn't dog you out like that! I'm a professional, baby!"

I loved that guy. He often drove me crazy with his impetuous nature. But he was as real as they came. So rare in Southern California and a welcome surprise. But, not-so-sadly, it was quickly coming to an end.

Right before I left the company, we were preparing for a round of layoffs, which included everyone I had suggested plus a couple of others I hadn't anticipated. Those felt retaliatory vs. substantive, but I was already halfway out the door and wholly uninterested in fighting anyone else's fight. If anything, I was happy that they too could extract themselves from the insanity I had experienced for the past four months. My boss' final knife twist came in the form of asking me to leave on the day that the termed employees were announced. I agreed as to not cause any unnecessary waves and to help prepare their exit packages and manage collecting equipment and company property on the day of. The final day rolled around. The conversations began first thing in the morning. Person after person was asked to join my boss in the curtained-off conference room and termination letters and severance packages were distributed. I joined them afterward, noticing the red faces and shell shock and collected any company property and oversaw their hurried packing of personal effects. It sucked. Just like it had at my previous jobs where I was the henchman. Once the termination conversations were completed, my boss had me quickly schedule an all-hands to discuss the terminations. I quickly realized that I was also being set up as one of the termed employees by perception when I had actually given notice two weeks prior and was aligning my last day with the attrition event.

"...and Phoenix is off to do his, um, furniture thing, right Phoenix?"

"Actually, I'm the new COO and Partner of a luxury home staging company."

I'd had enough of his bullshit. There's nothing more pathetic than a non-confident, weak, man in power who has zero self-awareness. Fuck that guy.

The second he was done speaking, I simply walked out. I had no desire to say goodbye or distribute hugs, not even to my own team. I may or may not have farted a little bit right before I got through the door as I left.

Lessons Learned

The Co-CEO thing doesn't work.

I believe the co-CEO thing is either a conspicuous cluster fuck or a cop out. Either there is a pissing contest playing out or someone doesn't have the balls to tell the other "I got this. Stand down." Simple as that. That particular situation was definitely a cluster fuck because the two CEOs were constantly at odds with one another and the morale of the team suffered tremendously because of it. Add to it the fact that their teams were in two separate locations often with edicts to stay away from the other's team. Explain to me how that's effective leadership starting at the top rung of the ladder? My job was made virtually impossible because I was constantly trying to navigate two sets of rules of engagement and two completely opposite, executive personalities. I pointed out during my interview that I got two completely different stories about the vision of the company and was essentially told I must have misunderstood each other's words. Are you fuckin' kidding me? No, he said X and you said Y...quite clearly. Explain.

I think co-CEOs is a dumb dynamic. Successful companies with co-founders have always created a hierarchy that's easy to follow and causes the least confusion for employees. Anything that creates confusion, especially if it erodes authority should be banished from the building.

Not everyone is cut out to be a CEO.

I personally thought the CEO I supported most was horrendous. Edicts were weak. Employees avoided him like the plague for fear of enduring yet another change of direction or sabotage attempt. He commanded zero respect from his team and was often too weak in his delivery to accomplish anything of significance. Hiring me was a great move until it wasn't. I tend to be pretty fearless and often claim the role of "the heavy" so that my bosses can skate through crunchy situations virtually unscathed. But when you rely on others to do your dirty work as CEO, you're essentially handing your credibility away as payment. And it's far too high a price to pay, especially in an early-stage company.

Not everyone is cut out to run a company successfully and command the respect necessary to do so. And that's okay. It's when CEOs who suck try to fit their square peg into a round hole and attempt to will their way to success without hiring a coach or mentor, listening more than they speak, and relying solely on what they've adopted that worked for their previous manager or what they read about in the leadership book du jour that the ecosystem becomes fraught with terrible CEOs. They have zero self-awareness, execute in silos, trust no one, and are apt to throw people under the bus regularly to avoid detection of their ineptitudes. Great CEOs are a rare breed. Not everyone will achieve greatness. And that's okay. There are plenty of other titles to choose from that take you directly out of the line of fire while maintaining a level of relevant (enough) power. Go that route.

Leave Gracefully

Even though I was over everything to do with my CEO, I still left gracefully. I made a trip to NYC that I really didn't need to make but did it to help the company save face and potentially score some lucrative projects down the road. I believed in the mission and the employees. Not the CEO, so my goal was to leave in a way that supported their continued success.

You MUST leave gracefully. Even if you've been treated like complete crap for months. Even if you have the world's best lawsuit waiting to be filed the day you walk out the door for the last time. Even if you have zero fucks left to give anyone in the company. You MUST leave gracefully.

In today's business climate your brand is everything. How you are perceived is incredibly important and directly relative to your success. If you are in a bad work situation it's important to do your best to divorce the emotion from the reality. When you're pissed/hurt/disappointed you tend to become reactionary vs. tactical. While you may be going through something individually, business continues. And since the business isn't only about you, you will be judged harshly for disrupting it in any way, even if you feel justified in doing so. The grand irony of life is that people have a long memory for the things you do wrong and an incredibly short memory for the things you do right. 10 years of stellar service can be wiped out with one bad experience. And that bad experience will be headline news for years to come. (Yelp, anyone?) EAs know this all too well. People love drama. And they love to excoriate and roast anyone who provides it.

It is important to walk away from even the worst situations with grace. Make sure that you're leaving having laid an easy-to-follow path for your successor. Be sure to remain painstakingly professional in your written and verbal conversations. Do not resort to gossip or disparaging your transgressor. As the English say, "Stiff upper lip and get on with it."

Business is all about optics. Managing your brand and allowing people to see you as a poised, unflappable, professional all the way to your final exit from the building gives them no opportunity to paint you as the bad guy. It allows you to leave with your head held high and protect your brand for your next employer. Lose your shit, start gossiping in the wings, slagging your soon-to-be ex-boss, and you will lose the respect of the people whom you will either need now for references and referrals or whom you will inevitably run into down the road. And you'll give the crows all the ammo they need to curse you for filth months after you're gone.

Don't be fooled. The business world is quite small and has fewer degrees of separation than you may think. I can go through my LinkedIn connections right now and within three degrees find someone I worked for or with whom I absolutely detested who is one degree away from my current boss. And since we list our company affiliations on LinkedIn it's not difficult to navigate and leverage these degrees of separation. Word travels fast in the shadows. Especially negative words. Worse, people make assumptions based on the facts they have, which may not even be all of the facts nor the most accurate ones. They go by their own experiences or a retelling of an experience they may have heard about, accurate or not. By maintaining your composure and leaving on good terms, as best you can, you're helping to write the narrative that will be shared numerous times behind your back and without your knowledge.

I remember walking into an interview with a CEO who proudly proclaimed that he'd looked at my LinkedIn, realized that I'd worked at company X for CEO Y, who just happened to be his next door neighbor, picked up the phone and called him and received a glowing review not from the CEO neighbor, but from his EA who, essentially, said I walk on water. Of course, I'm sitting there in shock and doing my best to navigate between emotions of unease and gratitude, with a little hint of suspicion about the person who would eventually become my new boss.

Even if you have every reason in the world to flame someone's insane behavior or a company's complicity with your suffering or a fellow employee's bullying and sabotage, don't. It's not worth it. For you, your brand, or your mental health. Focus on buttoning everything up to perfection, stepping your work game up another step (even when you want to check out), and go out in a blaze of glory vs. a barrage of accusations, excoriations, and character assassinations. It's not a good look. Ever.

This is one of my top questions: "What should I say in my exit interview?"

I keep it short, factual, and include absolutely nothing emotional or of real value. My real reasons for leaving the company are mine, if they aren't already obvious to everyone else. Since I've developed an insane lack of trust for HR, I tend to give them nothing that can be misconstrued or held against me. By the time the exit interview rolls around I've already laid a path for my successor, set my boss up for success for at least a month or two, and I simply want to beat a path out the door, get into my car, and get as far away from that place as possible, never to return. There is absolutely nothing more to talk about in an exit interview other than what steps I need to take to make sure my COBRA is enacted, company property is returned, and a polite handshake or hug is exchanged. I'm not interested in rehashing an issue that clearly wasn't solved while I was there and likely won't get solved once I leave. If it's enough of a problem to make me leave the company and they've done nothing to avoid the separation, figure it the fuck out yourself! I'm out!

The very last thing you want to do is be labeled as disgruntled or to bash people who still work every day at the company you're leaving. It can torpedo your brand and give people license to judge you or write you off as "good riddance," starting with HR. Like I say in my workshops, "When I leave, I leave potholes." No one can do what I do the way that I do it. And companies and executives realize how good they actually had it once I'm gone. That's the ultimate revenge. Not blasting a company or an exec on the way out the door.

THE END. FOR NOW.

Made in the USA
Columbia, SC
27 May 2021